THE KING'S SINGERS' MADRIGALS

Volume 1:

European Madrigals in 4 parts

DISTRIBUTED BY

7777 W. BLUEMOUND RD. P.O. BOX 13819 MILWAUKEE, WI 53213

First published in 1984 by Faber Music Ltd
in association with Faber & Faber Ltd
3 Queen Square London WC1N 3AU
Music drawn by James Holmes
Printed in USA

Music editor: Clifford Bartlett
German texts translated by Olive Sayce
Spanish text edited and translated by Jack Sage
Italian and French texts edited and translated by Sylvia Dimiziani,
Associate Professor of Music, State University of New York at Buffalo.

Grateful acknowledgment is given to the following for their advice:
Peter Butler, Peter Bartlett, Anthony Rooley and Professor Manlio Cortelazzo
of Centro di Studio per la Dialettologia Italiana, Padova.

A selection of these madrigals is recorded by the King's Singers on HMV
SLS 1078393 (2 record set), and also on tape cassette TC-SLS 1078395

CONTENTS

INTRODUCTION

The madrigal is perhaps the most satisfying form of music ever devised for recreational singing. This collection of 4-part pieces — together with the companion volume of 5-part pieces — has been drawn from the repertoire presented in the BBC Television series 'The King's Singers' Madrigal History Tour'. The choice was made to illustrate the enormous range of styles covered by the title Madrigal. It was not possible to include examples by all the best known composers, but we know that every piece in this volume is enjoyable to sing and can work well in performance.

The collection illustrates the development of the secular part-song from the Italian Frottola and Spanish Villancico of the late 15th century to the sophisticated contrapuntal style of the English madrigalists of the early 17th century. To music publishers of the period nearly all settings of secular verse came under the general heading of Madrigal, including sonnets, popular and dialect poems and ballets.

The Frottola was usually for solo voice with a simple, chordal accompaniment either for instruments or other voices. The words tended to be frivolous and often ribald. Gradually the more contrapuntal style of the Netherland composers — the *oltremontani*, men from the other side of the Alps — began to inspire a new generation of madrigal composers to seek to marry this style to the swift and supple rhythms of Italian poetry. Italy's greatest lyric poet, Petrarch, enjoyed a great revival during the 16th century and his expressive and flexible verse forms were used as models by poets and composers alike.

The first publications of madrigals in the 1530s and 1540s were highly successful, and revealed an avid market of literate and sophisticated people who relished the fashionable pastime of singing settings of poems about life and love. Each vocal line was now equally important, so that no-one with the necessary ability needed to feel left out at after-dinner entertainments.

Composers from Spain, Germany and France travelled to Italy to learn, or obtained published music to study. They adopted the madrigalists' musical style and applied it to their own vernacular poetry. In Spain the Villancico thrived well into the 16th century and was gradually developed polyphonically by Juan Vasquez and others. In Germany many composers set Italian texts as well as German (and sometimes a mixture of the two) and delighted in folk-song settings and satirical parodies. The French Chanson composers specialised in 'courtly love' songs and in lighter settings of the more frivolous aspects of love. In England the madrigal enjoyed a remarkable Indian Summer during the last years of the reign of Queen Elizabeth I, mainly due to the influence of one man, Thomas Morley. In his much-quoted book, *A Plaine and Easie Introduction to Practicall Musicke*, he outlined the qualities appropriate to both composers and performers of madrigals: They should be of 'an amorous humour . . . sometimes wanton, sometimes drooping, sometimes grave and staid . . . and the more variety [they] show the better [they] shall please!'

Many madrigals exist in more than one version, and in some cases the versions printed here are not precisely the same as those recorded by the King's Singers. They are notated with the convenience of today's singers in mind (see Editorial notes, p.71). For example, the time signature ¢ is used consistently to indicate a two-in-a-bar feel. Similarly, archaic spellings in the texts have generally been modernised. We would recommend a close reading of each text as a first priority: many of them are riddled with lascivious double-entendres which can be exploited effectively in performance. On the other hand, we have resisted the temptation to add tempo or dynamic indications, but we hope the brief Notes to each piece will assist singers in making their own decisions on the manner of performance. It is well worth experimenting with strongly contrasted vocal colours and dynamics. We suggest that vibrato is kept to a minimum.

William Byrd wrote: 'there is not any music of instruments whatsoever, comparable to that which is made of the voices of men, where voices are good, and the same well sorted and ordered'. While, as a male voice ensemble, we would agree with him, we freely admit that mixed voice ensembles are no less appropriate! In this collection, therefore, all the pieces are set at pitches suitable for SATB choirs and vocal groups.

Simon Carrington

The King's Singers
September 1983

PERFORMANCE NOTES AND TRANSLATIONS

1. *Dingaring, dingaring, dingaringadong, dingaringading.* (1) I got up one fine morning, one morning over the meadow; I met the nightingale singing beneath the branches. (2) I met the nightingale singing beneath the branches. 'Nightingale, nightingale, carry this message for me.' (3) 'Nightingale, nightingale, carry this message for me. Tell my lover that I am now married.'

The refrain may represent a guitar strumming; more probably it is the sound of wedding bells, ironically emphasising the singer's predicament. (The nightingale was a Renaissance symbol for a philanderer.) A *moderato* tempo is appropriate; there need be no strict relationship between the speeds of the verse and the refrain, which can effectively be repeated at the beginning and the end. The text mixes Spanish and French words, and it is recommended that phrases such as 'Je me levé' are pronounced as French.

2. *Fatal news! Come all and hear! Cotal's wife is dead.* (1) He found her with a Spaniard alone in his house, and so he killed her. The Spaniard escaped by means of his sword and his cunning. (2) 'Watch out if I catch you, Mr Spaniard; on my bed I'll give you such a "weapon" as will become the refrain of a dirge sung again and again.'

A fast tempo and strong vocal colours are required here to stress the sense of alarm conveyed by the 'fatal news' of a *crime passionelle*. The text includes some Italian words — ogni, moglie, piglio — which are more easily pronounced as Italian.

3. *Cuckoo, cuckoo, cuckuckoo! Watch out you don't become one too!* (1) My friend, you should know that even the best of women are always dying to be done. Make sure you satisfy your wife. (2) My friend, you must be on your guard against being cuckolded at all times; if your wife goes out for a piss, go out with her too.

This musically witty Villancico demands very light and precise singing (a fast two-in-a-bar at the opening). The cuckoo, because of its habits of taking over another bird's nest, is a common symbol for a cuckold.

4. I've just come from the poplars, mother, from watching them sway in the breeze; from the poplars of Seville, from seeing my sweet beloved, from watching them sway in the breeze.

Vásquez's elegant polyphonic treatment of a well-known Spanish folk song is best sung with tender simplicity in smooth, flowing lines.

5. (1) O Elslein, my dear Elselein, how I wish I were with you; but two deep waters lie between you and me. (2) That brings me great pain, dearest and closest to my heart; I say with all my heart that it is a great misfortune to me. (3) Let's hope that time will end it; let's hope that happiness may enter, and all may turn out well, dearest Elselein.

This vocal harmonization of a popular tune sounds best if the top part — the melody line — bears principal responsibility for the words, while the three lower parts provide a quasi-instrumental accompaniment.

6. How glorious is our [drinking] glass, how pleasing to God. Raise it up! Come on, drink up till not a drop is left. Down the hatch! Now, that's all inside me. Three cheers for our glass!

This drinking song is a blatant parody of ecclesiastical chanting and should not be sung too beautifully! Both this and the following song come from a collection compiled by Georg Forster and are sometimes attributed to him. Forster was a friend of Luther, and evidently supported his view that the Catholic clergy had life far too good and deserved ridicule.

7. (1) We went off to the wars, and there got neither purse nor money. *Blast the trumpet — and blast you too, your lordships!* (2) We came to Sibentod, and there got neither wine nor bread. (3) We came to Friaul, and there we really got a bellyful!

Sung by a group of penniless mercenaries, this hard-luck story is anything but sophisticated. The opening phrase of each verse can be sung by a different member of the group. By the third verse, they should sound thoroughly disgruntled, as they blow 'raspberries' (*alami*) at 'your lordships' — referring either to their employers or, with heavy sarcasm, to the local peasantry. The accent need not be pure, and can contain a mixture of Italian and German.

8. *Lirum bililirum, li-lirum, lirum, lirum. Ah, play the muted strings. You hear me well, Pedrina — and not just out of duty.* (1) For six years I have loved you and been your faithful servant, but I'm still waiting for you, and I shall surely burst with love. Ah, don't give me more grief; you know very well that I speak the truth. (2) Do you remember when you pledged your trust so happily, and you swore on the Gospels that you wanted me as your suitor? With a quick letter I answered you with a sigh. (3) When I think of the time that has passed and how I've loved you in vain, I throw myself in desperation to the demons of hell; and if you don't come to my aid this winter, I shall leave you. (4) Ah traitor, how can you bear to see me live in such desperation? Give me at least an hour with you and I shall be completely satisfied. Send a sealed letter to your good, faithful servant.

A song of 'courtly love' — perhaps a courtly musician having fun at the expense of the peasantry? The original text, in the Bergamasque dialect, has been modified slightly so that the correct effect may be obtained by following the normal rules of Italian pronunciation (see p.72). To begin softly, as from the distance, works well in performance. The cross-rhythms between the three upper voices and the bass should be emphasised.

9. To the hunt, to the hunt; come on, everyone hurry! Come gladly to our hunt with pointers and hounds. Whoever wants to come must hurry. Don't wait for daybreak; sound the horn, master of the hunt, and hurry, hurry! — Over here, Balzan, Lion, Fasan, Falcon, Tristan, Pizon, Alan, Carbon! Call the hounds from the mountain, you blockhead! — Now you, Pezolo and Spagnolo, have a keen eye for the deer! It's yours, Augustino, and yours, Pasalingua! Look there, take it on your shoulders, so that the dogs cannot tear it.

This hunting song sounds well if sung with a bright sound and much relish of the various names. (In bars 45 and 47, be sure to accent the first syllable of the names Augustino and Pasalingua). The word repetitions need to be clearly accentuated to create the illusion of hunting sounds. The relationship between the time changes is not clear cut and can be treated flexibly.

10. The sweet white swan dies while singing, and I, while weeping, reach the end of my life. What a strange and different fate; for he dies comfortless, while I die a blissful death — a death which fills me with joy and desire. If I feel no other pain than this in dying, I should be content to die a thousand deaths a day.

A famous madrigal, which is a deceptively simple setting of a highly emotional poem. As so often in Renaissance poetry the word 'die' (*morire*) is used in two senses: to denote release from life and a release of a more sexual nature.

11. (1) O my dearest lady, I want to sing a song beneath your window. He's a good fellow, is a lancer. *Dong dong dong, derry derry dong dong dong dong.* (2) I pray you listen to me, for I sing well, and I yearn for you as a Greek for his capon. (3) When I go hunting with the falcon, I'll bring you a woodcock fat as a kidney. (4) If I can't speak with beautiful phrases, it's because I've not read Petrarch nor drunk from Helicon's springs. (5) But if you will have

me, I'll not be a slacker; I'll make love all night long, lunging like a ram.

A Serenade sung by a Lanzo — a German mercenary — in broken Italian. His intentions towards his lady become increasingly obvious as the piece progresses, and this should be reflected in the performance.

12. *How pleasant to play the game of getting it in.* (1) As I was out looking for amusement the other day, I met a comely maiden. Smiling sweetly, I tried to kiss her. She objects, but I press onward, saying 'Let yourself go, come on!' (2) When she refused, I should have let her go, but I held her closely, and smiling sweetly tried to kiss her. What a fuss she makes, wriggling around. 'Let yourself go, come on!'

A typically bawdy French chanson couched in playful musical terms. It is effective sung fast and lightly, with a stylistic difference between *his* increasing insistent requests and *her* coy refusal. Needless to say he finally has his way!

13. *La la la, I dare not say it; la la la, I shall tell you after all.* There is a man in our village who is jealous of his wife. He is not jealous without reason, for he is certainly a cuckold. He gets ready and takes her along to the market with him.

Gossips in the market place are passing round the latest scandal. Every now and then they break off and mutter "la la la" under their breath for fear of being overheard by passers-by. Best sung fast and lightly.

14. *Margot, go to work in the vineyards, go early to work in the vineyards.* (1) Coming back from Lorraine, I met three captains, in the vineyards, by the vine. (2) They called out 'homely maiden!' and shunned me like the plague, in the vineyards, by the vine. (3) They gave me a bouquet of marjoram to gain my favour, in the vineyards, by the vine. (4) If it flowers, I'll be queen, and if it dies, I'll have to forfeit, in the vineyards, by the vine.

This setting of a folk song, as popular today as it was in the 16th century, should be sung simply and not too slowly. The text is riddled with double-entendres open to a variety of interpretations. (The source contains two verses only and verses 3 and 4 are supplied from the related folk song *En passant par la Lorraine*).

15. *When a kind lover puts aside his nymph, he grows old all at once.* (1) While far from your sight, O solace of my heart, I spent all my youth in languor, always sullen and never at peace. (2) A moment was for me as the longest day, a single day like a month's long journey, and a month seemed to last a year. (3) Now that the present has brought us together, I am overcome with great joy, completely happy and never sorrowful. (4) Don't let the years go by in vain; let us taste the delights of the moment and enjoy the fruits of this great happiness that will quickly flee.

This is an elegant sample of '*vers mesuré*' — a stylised attempt to reflect the word stresses in the music. There is scope for rubato in the verses (*Chant*), but the refrain (*Rechant* or *Reprise*), should always be sung in a courtly, dance-like rhythm. A practical performing sequence is: 4-part Rechant, 6-part Reprise (in which the melody is in the second voice), verse, Rechant, verse, Rechant, etc., ending if possible with the 6-part Reprise.

16. *My husband is handsome and kind, my dear.* Two women from the same village were talking to each other: 'Do you have a good husband?' 'He is handsome and kind, my dear. He never angers me, nor does he beat me. He does the housework and feeds the chickens while I enjöy myself. Oh my dear, it makes me laugh when the chickens squawk — "Oh little chickie, what's the matter?" — He is handsome and kind, my dear.'

A gossip song (like No 13) which sounds best sung at a brisk tempo and very lightly. The words should be projected clearly and colourfully, particularly the conversational duets, and fun can be had with the chicken squawks!

17. In this delicate and witty Pastoral, the double-entendres need not be underlined but should not be overlooked. The tempo can be fast and sprightly, with the bass pedal notes treated almost as instrumental pizzicati. At bar 33 the relationship between duple and triple time is unambiguous in the original source, since the top part has a semibreve/whole note rest without a change of time signature. However, the changes are frequently interpreted as ♩=♩ In either case the triple time section ought not to lose its lilt. If there is more than one singer per part, the opening phrase is better sung by a solo voice.

18. The distinctly rustic feel of this piece can be heightened in performance if sung in an extrovert manner and perhaps in a rustic accent. The triple time section is strengthened if 'ho' has as much accent as 'heigh'. 'Chill = I will.

19. This allegorical street-seller's song emphasises that things of worth — e.g. the finer human characteristics such as fidelity — are often concealed beneath the most humble and unlikely exteriors. In verse 3 'turtles' are turtle doves, reputed to pair for life, and 'twins' are Gemini, the heavenly twins — both underlining the theme of constancy. The word 'orienst' in verse 2 is often amended to 'orient', but is probably a contraction of 'orientest' — most eastern, i.e. most valuable. The piece should be sung in a forthright and lively style, with changes of colour for the nobler sentiments.

20. This is essentially a lute song, even though solo and 4-voice versions are both included in the original edition. The lower three parts should therefore be sung discreetly as an accompaniment, allowing pride of place to the top, melody line. To improve the flow, bars 9-10 and 48-9 can be elided, i.e. the rests removed. The rhythmic interest may be increased by grouping the 'yet, yet, yet, yet' of the refrain in twos rather than threes where this is implied by the harmony. The poem is obviously highly suggestive and singers may care to reflect this in their performance.

21. The bitter-sweet quality of this stunningly beautiful work will be enhanced by an even balance between the voices and a relish of the difference between the major and minor tonalities.

1. Dindirín, dindirín

ANON
(c.1500)

13
En - - - - con - - - tré le rui - - - - - se - - - ñor Que can - - -
"Rui - - - - se - - - ñor, le rui - - - - se - - - ñor, Fác - - - - teme a -
Y dí - - - ga - - - - - lo a mon a - - - - mi Que je
En - - - - - con - - - tré le rui - - - - se - - - ñor Que can - - -
"Rui - - - - se - - - ñor, le rui - - - - - se - - - ñor, Fác - - - - teme a -
Y dí - - - ga - - - - - lo a mon a - - - - mi Que je
En - - - - con - - - - tré le rui - - - - - se - - - ñor Que can - - -
"Rui - - - - - se - - - - ñor, le rui - - - - - se - - - ñor, Fác - - - - teme a -
Y dí - - - ga - - - - - lo a mon a - - - - mi Que je
En - - - - - con - - - tré le rui - - - - - se - - - ñor Que can - - -
"Rui - - - - se - - - - ñor, le rui - - - - se - - - - ñor, Fác - - - - teme a -
Y dí - - - ga - - - - - lo a mon a - - - - mi Que je
18
D.C.
- ta - - - - - ba so la ra - - - - - - ma.
- ques - - - - ta em - - - - ba - - - - xa - - - - - ta."
ya só ma - - - - - ri - - - - ta - - - - - ta."
Din - - di - - - rin - - - dín.
- ta - - - - - ba so la ra - - - - - ma.
- ques - - - - ta em - - - - ba - - - - xa - - - - - ta."
ya só ma - - - - - ri - - - - ta - - - - - ta."
Din - - di - - - rin - - - dín.
- ta - - - - ba so la ra - - - - - ma.
- ques - - - - ta em - - - - ba - - - - xa - - - - - ta."
ya só ma - - - - ri - - - - ta - - - - - ta."
Din - - di - - - rin - - - dín.
- ta - - - - - ba so la ra - - - - - ma.
- ques - - - - - ta em - - - - - ba - - - - xa - - - - - - ta
ya só ma - - - - - ri - - - - - ta - - - - - - ta."
Din - - di - - - rin - - - dín.

2. Fatal la parte

JUAN DEL ENCINA
(1468 - c.1529)

11
1. Por - que l'ha tro - ba - - to Con un es - pa - ño - - lo En su ca - - sa so - - - lo,
2. "Guar - da si te pi - glio, Don es - pa - ño - le - - to, So - pra del mi let - - - to
1. Por - que l'ha tro - ba - - to Con un es - pa - ño - - lo En su ca - - sa so - - - lo,
2. "Guar - da si te pi - glio, Don es - pa - ño - le - - to, So - pra del mi let - - - to
1. Por - que l'ha tro - ba - - to Con un es - pa - ño - - lo En su ca - - sa so - - - lo,
2. "Guar - da si te pi - glio, Don es - pa - ño - le - - to, So - pra del mi let - - - to
1. Por que l'ha tro - ba - - to Con un es - pa - ño - - lo En su ca - - sa so - - - lo,
2. "Guar - da si te pi - glio, Don es - pa - ño - le - - to, So - pra del mi let - - - to

17
D.C.
Lue - go l'ha maz - za - - to. Lui se l'ha es - ca - pa - - to Por for - za y por ar - - - te.
Te fa - rò un mar - til - - lo Tal que en es - tre - bil - - lo Pian - ge - ràn le car - - - te."
Lue - go l'ha maz - za - - to. Lui se l'ha es - ca - pa - - to Por for - za y por ar - - - te.
Te fa - rò un mar - til - - lo Tal que en es - tre - bil - - lo Pian - ge - ràn le car - - - te."
Lue - go l'ha maz - za - - to. Lui se l'ha es - ca - pa - - to Por for - za y por ar - - - te.
Te fa - rò un mar - til - - lo Tal que en es - tre - bil - - lo Pian - ge - ràn le car - - - te."
Lue - go l'ha maz - za - - to. Lui se l'ha es - ca - pa - - to Por for - za y por ar - - - te.
Te fa - rò un mar - til - - lo Tal que en es - tre - bil - - lo Pian - ge - ràn le car - - - te."

3. Cucú, cucú!

JUAN DEL ENCINA
(1468 - c.1529)

4. De los álamos vengo

JUAN VASQUEZ
(c. 1510 - c.1560)

De los á - - - - la-mos, de los á - - la - -
De los á - - la-mos ven-go, ma - - - - - - dre, de los á - la - mos ven -
De los á - - - - - - la - mos
De los á - - - la-mos, de los á - la-mos ven - - - - - - - - - -

6
- mos ven - - - - - go, ma - - - - - - - - - - - - dre, De ver có-mo, de ver
- go, ma - - - - - - - - - - - - - - - dre, De ver có-mo los me - ne-a el ai - - - re,
ven - - - - go, ma - - - - - - - - - - - - dre, De ver
- go, ma - - - - - - - - - - - - - dre, De ver có-mo los me-ne-a el ai - - -

10
có-mo los me - - ne - a ___ el ai - - - - - - - - - - - re, De los
de ver có-mo los _ me - - - ne - - - - a el ai - - - - re, De los á - - - - la-mos,
có - mo los me - ne - - - - a el ai - - - - - - - - - - - re. De los
- re, de _ ver _ có-mo los me - - - - ne - - a el ai - - - - - - - re. De los á - la - mos ven - go,

14
á - - lamos vengo, ma - - dre, De ver
de los á - - - la - - - mos ___ ven - - go, ma - - - - - - - - - - dre, De ver có-mo los me-
á - - - - - la - - mos ven - - - - go, ma - - - - - - - - - dre,
ma - dre, de los á - la - mos ven - - - - - - go, ma - - - - - - - - - - dre,

18
có-mo los me-ne-a el ai - - - re, de ver có-mo los me - ne - a ___ el ai - - - - - - - - -
- ne-a el ai - - - re, de ver có-mo los _ me - - - ne - - a el ai - - - re,
De ver có - - - mo los me - ne - - - - - a el ai - - - - - - - - -
De ver có-mo los me - ne - - - a el ai - - - - - - - - -

22
- re, de ver có-mo, de ver có-mo los me - - - ne - a ___ el
de ver có-mo los me - ne-a el ai - - - re, de ver có-mo los _ me - - - ne - - - - a el
- re, de ver có - - mo los me - ne - - - - a el
- re, de ver có-mo los me-ne-a el ai - - - - re, de _ ver _ có-mo los me - - - - ne - -

26
ai - - - - - - - - - - - - re.
ai - - - - re. ___ De los á - - - - la - - mos de Se - - vi - - - - - - - - - - - - lla, de los
ai - - - - - - - - - - - - re.
- a el ai - - - - - - - - re. De los á - - - - - - la-mos de Se - - - - - - vi - - - - lla,

30
De los á - - - la-mos de _ Se - - - vi - - - - - - - - - - - - lla, de Se - - - vi - - - - - - - - - -
á - la-mos de Se-vi - - - - lla, de los á - - - la - - mos de _ Se - vi - - - - - - - -
De los á - - - - - - - la - mos de Se - - - - - - - - vi - - - - - - - - - -
De los á - la - mos de Se - - - - vi - - - - - - - - - - - -

34
- lla, De ver a mi lin-da, de ver a mi lin-da a- - - - -
- lla, De ver a mi lin-da a-mi - - - - - - - - - - - - - ga, De ver a mi lin- - - - da
- lla, De ver a mi
- lla, De ver a mi lin-da, de ver a mi lin - - - - - - - - - - da

38
- mi - ga, De ver có-mo los me-ne-a el ai- -
a - - - - mi - - - - - - - - - - - - - - ga, De ver có-mo los me - ne-a el ai - - - re,
lin - - - - da a - - mi - - - - - - - - - - ga, De ver
a - - - - - - - - - - - - mi - - - - - - - - - - - - - ga, De ver

42
- re, de ver có-mo los me - ne - a el ai - - - - - - - - - - re. De los
de ver có-mo los me - - - ne - a el ai - - - re. De los á - - - - - la - mos,
có - - mo los me - ne - - - - a el ai - - - - - - - - - - - - re. De los
có-mo los me-ne - - - - a el ai - - - - - - - - - - - - re. De los á - la-mos ven - go,

46
á - la-mos vengo, ma - - - dre,
de los á - - - la - - - mos ___ ven - - go, ma - - - - - - - - - - dre, De ver có-mo los me-
á - - - - - - la - - mos ven - - - - - go, ma - - - - - - - - - - - dre,
ma - dre, de los á - la - mos ven - - - - - - go, ma - - - - - - - - - - - dre, De ver

50
De ver cómo, de ver cómo los me - - ne - a ___ el ai - - - - - - - - - re, de ver
- ne-a el ai - re, de ver cómo los me - - ne - a el ___ ai - - - re, de ver cómo los me-
De ver có - mo los me - ne - - - a el ai - - - - - - - - re,
cómo los menea el ai - - re, de _ ver cómo los me - - - ne - - a el ai - - - - - re,

55
cómo los me-ne-a el ai - - - re, de ver cómo los me - ne - - a ___ el ai - - - - - - - - re.
- ne-a el ai - - - re, de ver cómo los _ me - - - ne - a el ai - - - re. ___
de ver có - - mo los me - ne - - - - a el ai - - - - - - - - - re.
de ver cómo los me - ne - - - a el ai - - - - - - - - - - re.

5. Ach Elslein, liebes Elselein

LUDWIG SENFL
(c.1486 - c.1543)

12
-ser Wohl zwi-schen dir und mir, So sein zwei
-zen, Hab's für groß Un-ge-fäll, Red' ich von
-den, Herz-lieb-stes El-se-lein, Sich in all's
zwi-schen dir und mir, So sein zwei
für groß Un-ge-fäll, Red' ich von
-lieb-stes El-se-lein, Sich in all's
zwi-schen dir und mir, So sein zwei
für groß Un-ge-fäll, Red' ich von
-lieb-stes El-se-lein, Sich in all's
-ser Wohl zwi-schen dir und mir, So sein zwei tie-
-zen, Hab's für groß Un-ge-fäll, Red' ich von gan-
-den, Herz-lieb-stes El-se-lein, Sich in all's Güts

18
tie-fe Was-ser Wohl zwi-schen dir und mir.
gan-zem Her-zen, Hab's für groß Un-ge-fäll.
Güts ver-wen-den, Herz-lieb-stes El-se-lein.
tie-fe Was-ser Wohl zwi-schen dir und mir.
gan-zem Her-zen, Hab's für groß Un-ge-fäll.
Güts ver-wen-den, Herz-lieb-stes El-se-lein.
tie-fe Was-ser Wohl zwi-schen dir und mir.
gan-zem Her-zen, Hab's für groß Un-ge-fäll.
Güts ver-wen-den, Herz-lieb-stes El-se-lein.
-fe Was-ser Wohl zwi-schen dir und mir.
-zem Her-zen, Hab's für groß Un-ge-fäll.
ver-wen-den, Herz-lieb-stes El-se-lein.

6. Vitrum nostrum gloriosum

ANON
(1540)

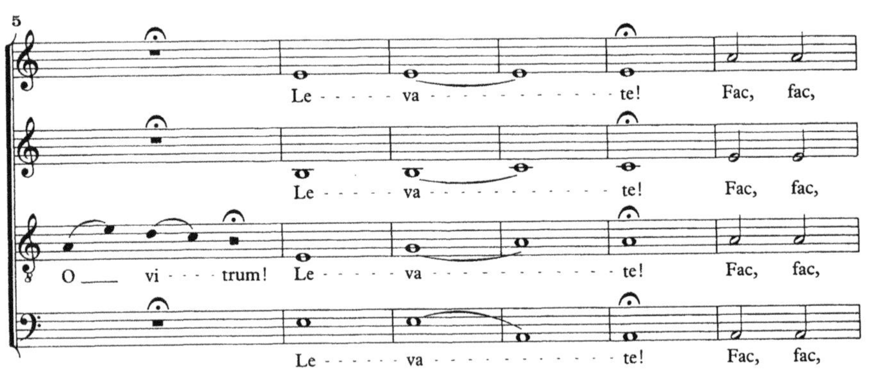

16
bi - be to - tum ex - - - - tra, ut ni - hil ma - ne - at in - - - tra. De - - - -
bi - be to - tum ex - - - - tra, ut ni - hil ma - ne - at in - - - tra. De - - - -
bi - be to - tum ex - - - - tra, ut ni - hil ma - ne - at in - - - tra. De - - - -
bi - be to - tum ex - - - - tra, ut ni - hil ma - ne - at in - - - tra. De - - - -

21
- po - - - - - - - - - - ne! Pro - se - - qua - mur
- po - - - - - - - - - - ne! Pro - se - - qua - mur
- po - - - - - - - - - - ne! Hoc est in vi - sce - ri - bus me - is. Pro - se - - qua - mur
- po - - - - - - - - - - ne! Pro - se - - qua - mur

27
lau - - - - - - - - - - de, pro - - - - - - - - se - - - qua - - mur lau - - - - - de!
lau - - - - - - - - - - - - - de, pro - - se - - - qua - - mur lau - - - - - de!
lau - - - - - - - - - - - de!
lau - - - - - - - - - - - - de, pro - - - - - - - - se - - - qua - - mur lau - - - - - de!

7. Wir zogen in das Feld

ANON
(1540)

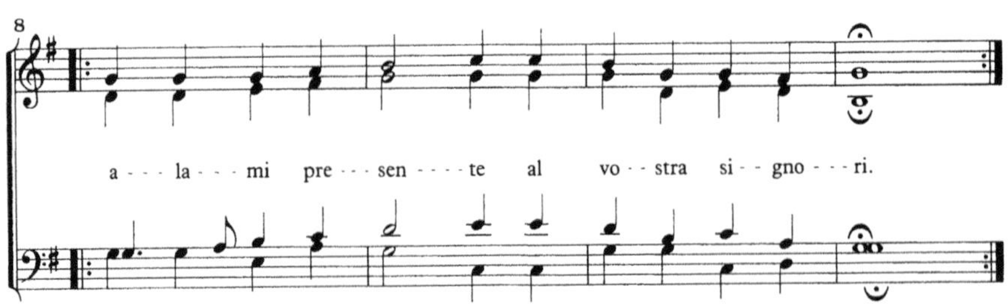

8. Lirum bililirum

ROSSINO MANTOVANO
(fl.1510)

14
Li - rum bi - li - li - - rum, bi - li - li - rum, li - li - rum, li - rum, li - - - - rum. Deh, si so - ni
Li - rum bi - li - li - - rum, bi - li - li - rum, li - li - rum, ___ li - rum. ___ Deh, si so - ni ___
Li - rum bi - li - li - - rum, bi - li - li - rum, li - rum, li - rum, li - - - - rum. Deh, si ___ so - ni
Li - - - rum bi - - - - li - - - - - - li - - - rum, li - - - rum. Deh, si so - - - -

19
la ___ sor - - - - di - - na, deh, si so - - - - - ni la sor - - di - - - - - na.
la ___ sor - - di - - na, deh, si so - ni la sor - - - - di - - - - - na.
la sor - - - - di - - - na, ___ deh, si so - - - - - - ni la sor - - - - di - - - - - - na.
- ni la sor - di - - - na, deh, si so - - - - - - ni la sor - - di - - - - - - na.

25
1. Les ses an che t'vo mi ___ ben E che t'son bon ___
2. Ta re - cor - det quant t'me ___ des La tua fè si ___
1. Les ses an che t'vo mi ben ___ E bon
2. Ta re - cor - det quant t'me des ___ La fè a - - - - - -
1. Les ses an che t'vo ___ mi ben ___ E che t'son bon
2. Ta re - cor - det quant ___ t'me des ___ La tua fè si
1. Les ses an che t'vo mi ben ___ E bon
2. Ta re - cor - det quant t'me des ___ La fè a - - - - - -

29
ser - vi - - - - - - - - - dor, Ma t'a - spet che l'so ben
a - - le - - - - gra - - met, E ch'ai Van - gel t'me giu - - - - - - - - res
ser - - - - vi - - - - - - dor, Ma t'a - spet che l'so ben
- le - - - - gra - - - - - met, E ch'ai Van - gel t'me giu - - - - res
ser - vi - - - - - - - - - dor, Ma t'a - spet che l'so ben
a - - le - gra - - - - - met, E ch'ai Van - gel t'me giu - - - - res
ser - - - - vi - - - - - - dor, Ma t'a - spet che l'so ben
- le - - - - gra - - - - - - met, E ch'ai Van - gel t'me giu - - - - - res
34
Ch'al fin sclo - pi per a - - - - - - - mor. Deh, non da plu tat do - - - -
De vo - lim per to ser - - - - - - - - vet? Mi per lit - - - ra in - con - ti - - - - -
Ch'al fin per a - - - - - - mor. Deh, non da plu tat do - -
De vo - - - - - - lim ser - - - - - - vet? Mi per lit - - - ra in - con - - - - ti - -
Ch'al fin sclo - - - pi per a - - - - - - - - - mor. Deh, non da plu tat do - - - -
De vo - lim per to ser - - - - - - - - vet? Mi per lit - - - ra in - con - ti - - - -
Ch'al fin per a - - - - - - mor. Deh, non da plu tat do - -
De vo - - - - - - lim ser - - - - - - vet? Mi per lit - - - ra in - - - con - ti - -
39
- lor, Tu sa ben che dig il vi - rum.
- net A t're - spo - - - - - si cum su - - - spi - rum.
- lor, Tu sa ben che dig il vi - - - - - - rum.
- net A t're - spo - - - - - si cum su - - - - - spi - - - - - - rum.
- lor, Tu sa ben che dig il vi - rum.
- net A t're - spo - - - - - si cum su - - - - - spi - rum.
- lor, Tu sa ben che dig il vi - - - - - - rum.
- net A t're - spo - - - - - - si cum su - - - spi - - - - - - rum.

43
Li-rum bi-li-li - rum, bi-li-li-rum, li - li-rum, li-rum, li - - - - rum. Deh, si so - ni
Li - rum bi-li-li - rum, bi-li-li-rum, li - li - rum, li - rum. Deh, si so - ni
Li-rum bi-li-li - rum, bi-li-li-rum, li-rum, li-rum, li - - - - rum. Deh, si so - ni
Li - - - rum bi - - - - li - - - - - li - - - -rum, li - - - rum. Deh, si so - - - -

48
Fine
la sor - - - - di - - - na, deh, si so - - - - - - ni la sor - - di - - - - - - na.
la sor - - di - - - na, deh, si so - ni la sor - - - - - di - - - - - - na.
la sor - - - - di - - - na, deh, si so - - - - - - ni la sor - - - - di - - - - - - na.
- ni la sor - - di - - - na, deh, si so - - - - - - ni la sor - - di - - - - - - na.

54
3. Quant a - pen - si al temp pas - - - - - - - - - sat E che to ser - - -
4. Com' po t'mai sof - - - fri, trai - - - - - to - - - ra, Che c'sì vi - - vi
3. Quant a - - pen - si al temp pas - - - - - sat E
4. Com' po t'mai sof - - - fri, trai - - - - - to - - - - - ra, Che c'sì
3. Quant a - - pen - si al temp pas - - - - - - sat E che to ser -
4. Com' po t'mai sof - - - fri, trai - - - - - - to - - - - - - - - - ra, Che c'sì vi - - - - vi
3. Quant a - - pen - si al temp pas - - - - - sat E
4. Com' po t'mai sof - - - fri, trai - - - - - to - - - - - ra, Che c'sì

58
vi - ta in - - - dà - - ren, A m'do - ni de - - - spe - - - - - - - - - - - - rat
di - spe - - - - - - - - rat? Da m'au - den - za al - mac un ho - - - - ra
in - - - - dà - - - - - ren, A m'do - ni de - - spe - - - - - - - - - - - - rat
di - - - - spe - - - - - - rat? Da m'au - den - za al - mac un ho - - - - ra
vi - ta in - dà - - - - - - ren, A m'do - ni de - - - spe - - - - - - - - - - - - - rat
di - spe - - - - - - - - - rat? Da m'au - den - za al - mac un ho - - - - - - - - ra
in - - - - dà - - - - - - ren, A m'do - ni de - - spe - - - - - - - - - - - - rat
di - - - - spe - - - - - - rat? Da m'au - den - za al - mac un ho - - - - ra
63
Al de - mo - ni da l'in - - - - - fe - - - ren. Ma s'non m'aidi ques in - ve - - - - -
Che se - - rò al tut a - - - - - pa - - - gat. Fa m'un scrit e su - - - -
Al l'in - - - - fe - - - - - - ren. Ma s'non m'aidi ques in - - - - ve - -
Che tut a - - - - - - pa - - - - - - gat. Fa m'un scrit e su -
Al de - mo - - - ni da l'in - fe - - - - - - ren. Ma s'non m'aidi ques in - ve - - - - -
Che se - - rò al tut a - - pa - - - - - - gat. Fa m'un scrit e su - - - -
Al l'in - - - - fe - - - - - - ren. Ma s'non m'aidi ques in - ve - -
Che tut a - - - - - pa - - - - - - gat. Fa m'un scrit e su - - - - -
68
- ren E mi vo da te par - - - ti - - rum.
- glat Del mio bon fi - - del ser - - - vi - - rum.
- ren E mi vo da te par - - - - - - ti - - - - - - rum.
- glat Del mio bon fi - - del ser - - - - - - vi - - - - - - rum.
- ren E mi vo da te par - - - - - - ti - - rum.
- glat Del mio bon fi - - del ser - - - - - vi - - rum.
- ren E mi vo da te par - - - ti - - - - - - rum.
- glat Del mio bon fi - - - - - del ser - - - vi - - - - - - rum.

9. Alla cazza

ANON
(c.1500)

18
spaz - za. Non ___ a - - - - - spet - tar il gior - no. Suo - na il cor - no, o ca - po di caz - za,
spaz - za. Non a - - - - - spet - tar il gior - no. Suo - na il cor - no, o ca - po di caz - za, e
spaz - za. Non a - - - - spet - tar il gior - no. E
spaz - za. Non a - - - - - spet - tar il gior - no. E

23
e spazza, spazza, spaz - - - - za.
spazza, spaz - za, spaz - za, e spazza, spaz - za, spaz - za, e spazza, spazza, spaz - - - - - za.
spazza, spaz - za, spaz - za, e spazza, spaz - za, spaz - za, e spazza, spazza, spaz - - - - - za.
spazza, spaz - za, spaz - za, e spazza, spaz - za, spaz - za, e spazza, spazza, spaz - - - - - za.

27
Te qui, Balzan, te qui, Li - on, Te qui, Fa - san, te qui, Fal - con, Te qui, Tristan, te
Te qui, Balzan, te qui, Li - on, Te qui, Fa - san, te qui, Fal - con, Te qui, Tristan, te
Te qui, Balzan, te qui, Li - on, Te, te qui, Fa - san, te qui, Fal - con, Te, te qui, Tristan, te
Te qui, Balzan, te qui, Li - on, Te qui, Fa - san, te qui, Fal - con, Te, te qui, Tristan, te

32
qui, Pi-zon, Te qui, A-lan, te qui, Car - bon. Chia - - ma li brac - chi dal
qui, Pi-zon, Te qui, A-lan, te qui, Car - bon. Chia - - ma li brac - chi dal
qui, Pi-zon, Te, te qui, A-lan, te qui, Car - bon. Chia - - ma li brac - chi dal
qui, Pi-zon, Te qui, A-lan, te qui, Car - bon. Chia - - ma li brac - chi dal

37
mon - te, bab-bi - - - on. Te qui, Pe - zo - - lo,
mon - te, bab-bi - - - on. Te qui, Pe - zo - - lo, te qui, Spa-gno - lo,
mon - te, bab-bi - - - on. Te, te qui, Pe - zo - - lo, te qui, Pe - zo - - lo, te qui, Spa-gno - lo,
mon - te, bab-bi - - - on. Te, te qui, Pe - zo - - lo, te qui, Pe - zo - - lo, te qui, Spa-gno - lo,

41
te qui, Spa-gno - lo, Ab-bi buon oc-chio al ca - - pri - - o - - - - lo. A te, Au-gu - sti - -
Ab-bi buon oc-chio al ca - - pri - - o - - - - lo. A te, Au-gu - sti - -
te qui, Spa-gno - lo, Ab-bi buon oc-chio al ca - - pri - - o - - - - lo. A te, Au-gu - sti - -
te qui, Spa-gno - lo, Ab-bi buon oc-chio al ca - - pri - - o - - - - lo. A te, Au-gu - sti - -

46
-no, a te, a te, Pa-sa-lin--gua. Vi-de là, vi-de là, vi-de là, vi-de là, vi---de
-no, a te, a te, Pa-sa-lin--gua. Vi-de là, vi-de là, vi-de là, vi-de là, vi---de
-no, a te, a te, Pa-sa-lin--gua. Vi-de là, vi-de là, vi-de là, vi-de là, vi-de là,
-no, a te, a te, Pa-sa-lin--gua. Vi-de là, vi-de là, vi-de là, vi-de là, vi-de là,

51
là, vi---de là. A spal-la, a spal-la pi-glia, pi-glia---la,
là, vi---de là. A spal-la, a spal-la pi------glia---la,
vi------de là. A spal-la, a spal-la pi------glia---la,
vi------de là. A spal-la, a spal-la pi-glia, pi-glia---la,

56
Che li ca-----ni non la straz------za.
Che li ca-----ni non la straz------za.
Che li ca-----ni non la straz------za.
Che li ca-----ni non la straz-------za.

10. Il bianco e dolce cigno

ALFONSO d'AVALOS
(1502 - 1544)

JACQUES ARCADELT
(c.1505 - 1568)

16
e di - - ver - sa sor - - te, Ch'ei mo - re scon - so - - la - to, Ed io mo - ro be -
e di - ver - sa sor - - te, Ch'ei mo - - - - re scon - so - la - to, Ed io mo -
e di - ver - sa sor - te, Ch'ei mo - re scon - so - la - to, Ed io mo -
Stran' e di - ver - sa sor - te,

21
- a - - - - - - - - - - - - - - - - - to. Mor - - - - te che nel mo -
- ro be - - a - to. Mor - te che nel mo -
- ro ed io mo - ro be - - - a - - - - - - - - - - to. Mor - te che nel mo -
Ed io mo - - ro be - a - - - - - - - - - - - - - - - - to. Mor - te che nel mo -

26
- ri - - - re, M'em - pie di gio - ia tut - t' e di de - - si - - - - - re. Se nel mo - rir'
- ri - - - re, M'em - pie di gio - ia tut - t' e di de - - - - si - - re. Se nel mo - rir'
- ri - - - re, M'em - pie di gio - ia tut - t' e di de - si - - - - - re. Se nel mo - rir'
- ri - - - re, M'em - pie di gio - ia tut - t' e di de - - si - - - - - re. Se nel mo - rir'

32
__ al - tro do - - - lor non sen - - - - to, ______ Di mil - - - le
__ al - tro do - lor non sen - to, Di mil - - - le morte il di, di mil - - - - - - le
__ al - tro do - - - lor non sen - - - - to, Di mil - - - le mor - - te il di, di mil - - - le
__ al - tro do - - - lor non sen - - - - to, Di mil - - - le mor - - te il di ___

37
morte il di sa - rei conten - - - - - - - to, di mil - - le morte il di sa -
morte il di, di mil - - le mor - te il di, di mil - - - - - - le morte il di,
mor - te il di sa - rei con-ten-to, di mil - - - le mor - te il di, di mil - - le mor - te il di sa -
__ sa - - - - rei con-ten - - - - - to, di mil - - - le mor - te il di ______ sa - - - -

42
- rei conten - - - - - - - - to. ______
di mil - - - le mor - - te il di sa - - - rei ______ con - ten - - - to.
- rei con-ten - - - - - - to, di mil - - - le mor - - te il di sa - rei con-ten - - - to.
- rei con-ten - to, di mil - - - le mor - - te il di sa - - - rei con-ten - - - to.

11. Matona, mia cara

ORLANDO DE LASSUS
(1532 - 1594)

13
-tar sot-to fi - - ne - - stra, Lan - - - tze buon com - - pa - gnon. Don don don, di-ri di-ri
-tar sot-to fi - - ne - stra, Lan - - - tze buon com - pa - - - - - - - gnon. Don don don, di-ri di-ri
-tar sot-to fi - - ne - stra, Lan - - tze buon com-pa - - - gnon. Don don don, di-ri di-ri
-tar sot-to fi - - ne - stra, Lan - - tze buon com - - pa - - - gnon. Don don don, di-ri di-ri

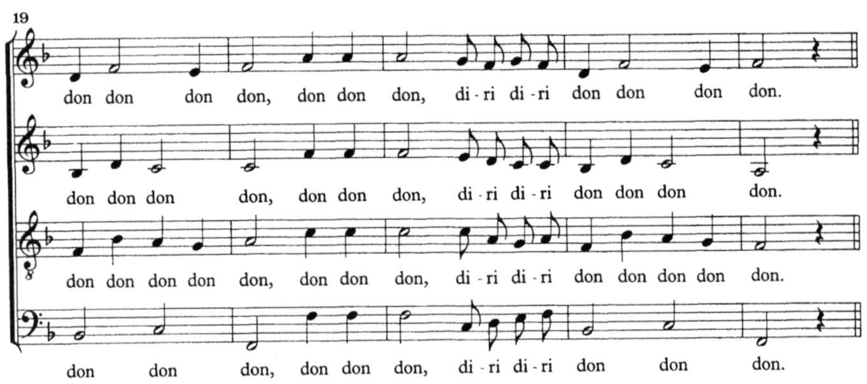
19
don don don don, don don don, di - ri di - ri don don don don.
don don don don, don don don, di - ri di - ri don don don don.
don don don don don, don don don, di - ri di - ri don don don don don.
don don don, don don don, di - ri di - ri don don don.

(23)
Ti pre - go m'a - scol - - ta - - - re, Che mi can - tar de bon,
Ti pre - go m'a - scol - - ta - - - re, Che mi can - - - - tar de bon,
Ti pre - go m'a - scol - - ta - - - re, Che mi can - - - - tar de bon,
Ti pre - go m'a - scol - - ta - - - re, Che mi can - - tar de bon,

(28)
E mi ti fol - ler be - - - - - - ne, Co - - - me gre - - co e ca - - - - - pon. Don don
E mi ti fol - ler be - - - ne, Co - - - me gre - co e ca - - - - - pon. Don don
E mi ti fol - ler be - - - ne, Co - - - - - me gre - - - - co e ca - - - - - - - - pon. Don don
E mi ti fol - ler be - - ne, Co - - - me gre - - co e ca - - - - pon. Don don

34
don, di-ri di-ri don don don don, don don don, di-ri di-ri don don don don.
don, di-ri di-ri don don don don, don don don, di-ri di-ri don don don don.
don, di-ri di-ri don don don don don, don don don, di-ri di-ri don don don don don.
don, di-ri di-ri don don don, don don don, di-ri di-ri don don don.

(39)
Com' andar al - le caz - ze, Caz - zar, caz - zar con le fal - - - con,
Com' andar al - le caz - ze, Caz - zar, caz - zar con le fal - con,
Com' andar al - le caz - ze, Caz - zar, caz - zar con le fal - - - con,
Com' andar al - le caz - ze, Caz - zar, caz - zar con le fal - - - con,

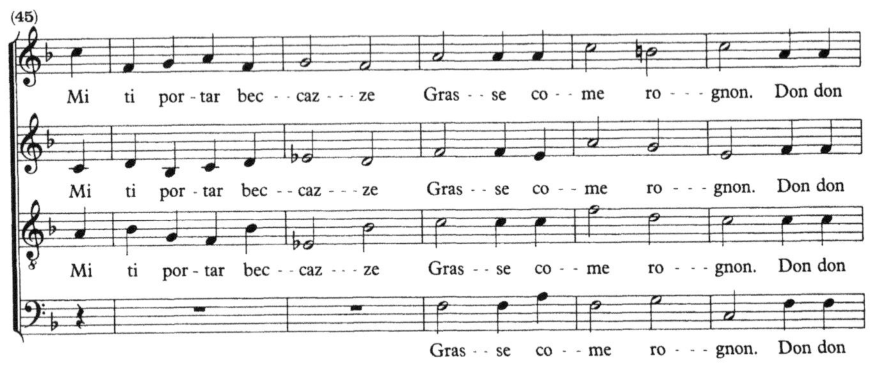
(45)
Mi ti por-tar bec--caz---ze Gras--se co--me ro---gnon. Don don
Mi ti por-tar bec--caz---ze Gras--se co--me ro---gnon. Don don
Mi ti por-tar bec--caz---ze Gras--se co--me ro---gnon. Don don
Gras--se co--me ro---gnon. Don don

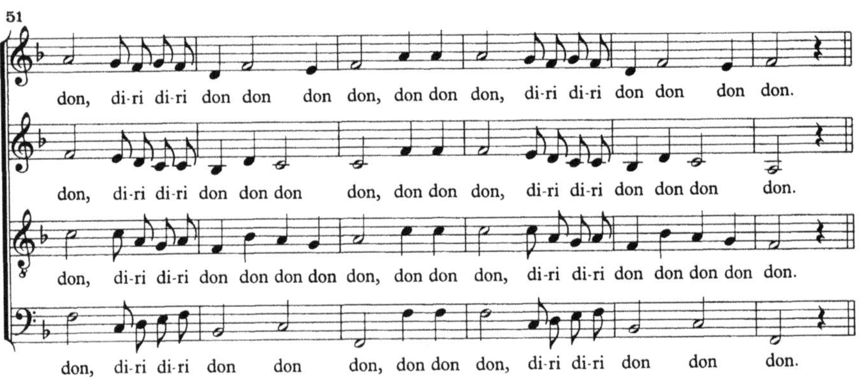
51
don, di-ri di-ri don don don don, don don don, di-ri di-ri don don don don.
don, di-ri di-ri don don don don, don don don, di-ri di-ri don don don don.
don, di-ri di-ri don don don don don, don don don, di-ri di-ri don don don don don.
don, di-ri di-ri don don don, don don don, di-ri di-ri don don don.

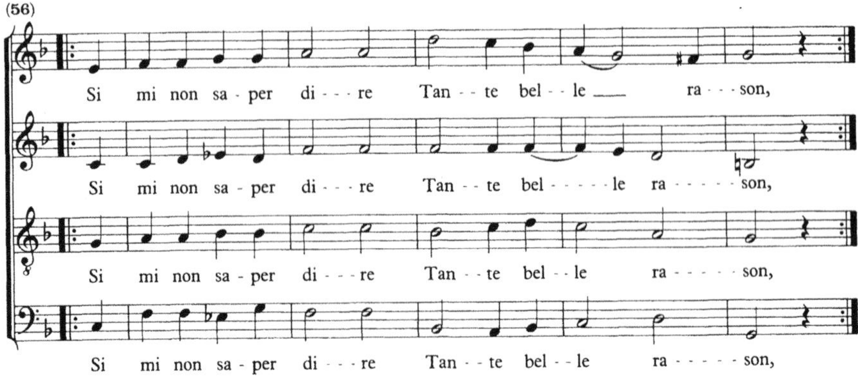
(56)
Si mi non sa-per di---re Tan--te bel--le ra---son,
Si mi non sa-per di---re Tan--te bel-----le ra-----son,
Si mi non sa-per di---re Tan--te bel--le ra-----son,
Si mi non sa-per di---re Tan--te bel--le ra-----son,

(61)
Pe - - trar - cha mi ___ non sa - - - - per, Ne fon - - - te d'He - - - - li - - con. Don don
Pe - - trar - cha mi ___ non sa - - - per, Ne ___ fon - te d'He - li - - - - - con. Don don
Pe - - trar - cha mi ___ non sa - - - per, Ne fon - - - te d'He - li - - - - - con. Don don
Pe - - trar - cha mi ___ non sa - - - per, Ne fon - - - te d'He - li - - - - con. Don don

68
don, di-ri di-ri don don don don, don don don, di-ri di-ri don don don don.
don, di-ri di-ri don don don don, don don don, di-ri di-ri don don don don.
don, di-ri di-ri don don don don don, don don don, di-ri di-ri don don don don don.
don, di-ri di-ri don don don, don don don, di-ri di-ri don don don.

(73)
Se ti mi fol - ler be - - - - ne, Mi non es - - ser pol - - - tron,
Se ti mi fol - ler be - - - - ne, Mi non es - - - - ser pol - - - tron,
Se ti mi fol - ler be - - - - - - - ne, Mi non es - - - - ser pol - tron,
Se ti mi fol - ler be - - - - ne, Mi non es - - - - ser pol - - - tron,

(79)
Mi fic - car tut - ta not - - - - te, Ur - tar, ur - tar, co - me mon -
Mi fic - car tut - - - - ta not - te, Ur - - tar, ur - - - tar, ur - - tar, co - me mon -
Mi fic - car tut - ta not - - - - te, Ur - - tar, ur - - - tar, ur - - tar, co - me mon-
Mi fic - car tut - ta not - - - - te, Ur - tar, ur - tar, co - - - me mon-

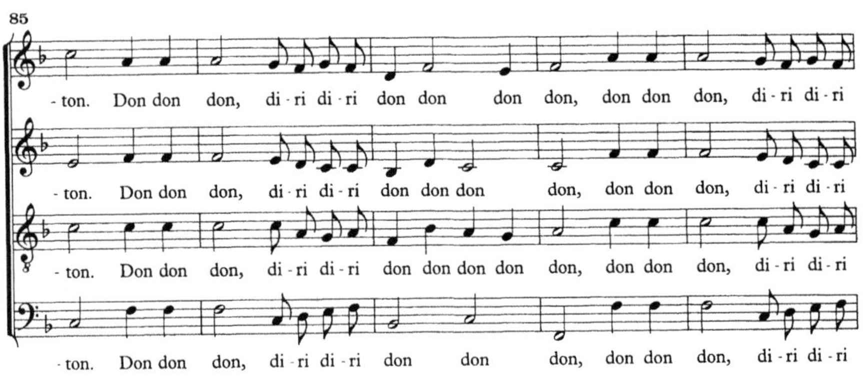
85
- ton. Don don don, di - ri di - ri don don don don, don don don, di - ri di - ri
- ton. Don don don, di - ri di - ri don don don don, don don don, di - ri di - ri
- ton. Don don don, di - ri di - ri don don don don don, don don don, di - ri di - ri
- ton. Don don don, di - ri di - ri don don don, don don don, di - ri di - ri

90
don don don don, don don don don don don.
don don don don, don don don don don don.
don don don don don, don don don.
don don don, don don don, don don don don don don don don.

12. Au joli jeu

CLEMENT JANEQUIN
(c.1485 - 1558)

11
- trier m'a-loi - - - - - e é - ba - loi - - er, l'au -
un re - fus me faut lais - ser, pour
- trier m'a-loi - - - - - e é - ba - loi - - er, l'au -
un re - fus me faut lais - ser, pour
1. L'au-trier m'a - loi - - - - - e é - - ba - loi - er,
2. Pour un re - - fus me faut lais-ser,
1. L'au-trier m'a - loi - - - - e é - - ba - loi - er,
2. Pour un re - - fus me faut lais-ser,
16
- trier m'a - loi - - - - - e é - ba - loi - - er, Je rencontrai la belle au corps gent, Sou-ri-ant
un re - fus me faut lais - ser, Propos lui tiens a - mou-reu - se - ment, Sou-ri-ant
- trier m'a loi - - - - - e é - ba - loi - - er, Je rencontrai la belle au corps gent, Sou-ri-ant
un re - fus me faut lais - ser, Propos lui tiens a - mou-reu - se - ment, Sou-ri-ant
Je rencontrai la belle au corps gent, Sou-ri-ant
Propos lui tiens a - mou-reu - se - ment, Sou-ri-ant
Je rencontrai la belle au corps gent, Sou-ri-ant
Propos lui tiens a - mou-reu - se - ment, Sou-ri-ant
21
doucement, la voix bai - - - ser. Elle en fait dou - te, Mais je la bou - te,
doucement, la voix bai - - - ser. El - - le ri - ot - te, Dan-ce sans not - te,
doucement, la voix bai - ser. Elle en fait dou - te, Mais je la bou - te,
doucement, la voix bai - ser. El - - le ri - ot - - te, Dan-ce sans not - te,
doucement, la voix bai - ser. Elle en fait dou - - te, Mais je la bou - te, Et
doucement, la voix bai - ser. El - - le ri - ot - - - te, Dan-ce sans not - te,
doucement, la voix bai - - - ser. Elle en fait dou - - te, Mais je la bou - te, Et
doucement, la voix bai - - - ser. El - - le ri - ot - - - te, Dan-ce sans not - te,

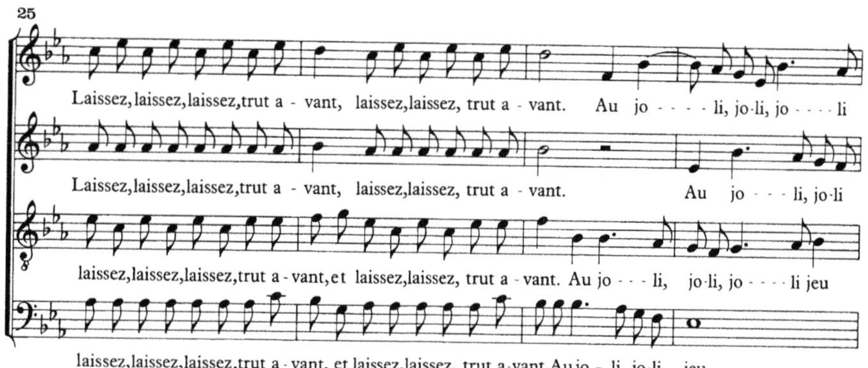
25
Laissez, laissez, laissez, trut a - vant, laissez, laissez, trut a - vant. Au jo - - - - li, jo-li, jo - - - - li
Laissez, laissez, laissez, trut a - vant, laissez, laissez, trut a - vant. Au jo - - - li, jo-li
laissez, laissez, laissez, trut a - vant, et laissez, laissez, trut a - vant. Au jo - - - li, jo-li, jo - - - - li jeu
laissez, laissez, laissez, trut a - vant, et laissez, laissez, trut a-vant. Au jo - li, jo-li jeu

29
jeu du pousse a - vant, du pousse a - - vant, au jo - - - - - li, jo-li, jo - - - - li
jeu du pousse a - vant, du pousse a - vant, pousse a-vant, au jo - - - - li, jo-li
du pousse a - - - - vant, du pousse a - vant, au jo - - - - li, jo-li, jo - - - - li jeu
du pousse a - - vant, du pousse a - vant, au jo - - - - li, jo-li jeu

33
1.
2.
jeu du pousse a - vant, du pousse a - - vant Il fait bon jou - er. 2. Pour - er.
jeu du pousse a-vant du pousse a - vant, Il fait bon jou - er. 2. Pour - er.
du pousse a - - - vant, du pousse a - vant fait bon jou - - - - er. - er.
du pousse a - vant fait bon jou - - er. - er.

13. La la la, je ne l'ose dire

PIERRE CERTON
(c.1500 - 1572)

12
Il n'est pas ja - - - loux sans cau - se, Mais il est co - - - cu du tout.
Il a - - prê - te et si la mai - ne Au mar-ché s'en va à tout.
Et
Il n'est pas ja - - - loux sans cau - se, Mais il est co - - - cu du tout.
Il a - - prê - te et si la mai - ne Au mar - - ché s'en va à tout.
Et
Il n'est pas ja - - - loux sans cau - se, Mais il est co - - - cu du tout.
Il a - - prê - te et si la mai - ne Au mar - - ché s'en va à tout.
Et
Il n'est pas ja - - - loux sans cau - se, Mais il est co - - - cu du tout.
Il a - - prê - te et si la mai - ne Au mar - - ché s'en va à tout.
Et

16
la la la, je ne l'o-, je ne l'o-, je ne l'o - se di - - - re,
la la la, je ne l'o-, je ne l'o-, je ne l'o - se di - - - re,
la la la, je ne l'o-, je ne l'o-, je ne l'o - se di - - - re,
la la la, je ne l'o-, je ne l'o-, je ne l'o - se di - - - re,

19
La la la, je le vous di - rai, Et la la la, je le vous di - rai.
La la la, je le vous di - rai, Et la la la, je le vous di - rai.
La la la, je le vous di - rai, Et la la la, je le vous di - rai.
La la la, je le vous di - rai, Et la la la, je le vous di - rai.

14. Margot labourez les vignes

JACQUES ARCADELT
(c.1500 - 1568)

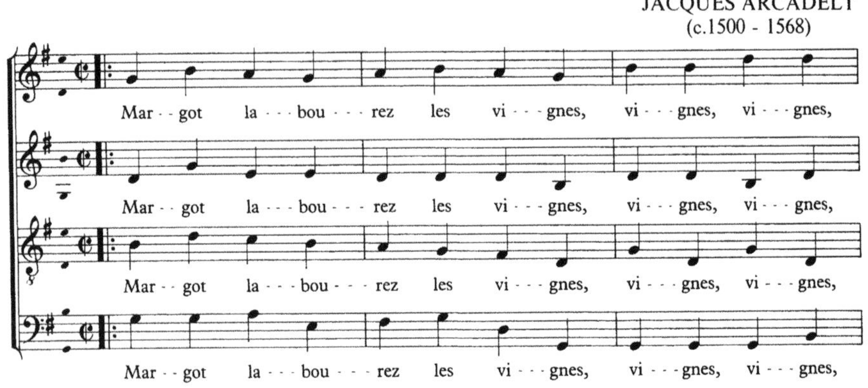

11
En re - - - ve - - - nant de Lor - - - rai - - - ne, Mar - - - - - - got,
Ils m'ont sal - - - u - - - - é vi - - - lai - - - ne, Mar - - - - - - got,
En re - - - ve - - - nant de Lor - - - rai - - - ne, Mar - - got, Ren - - -
Ils m'ont sal - - - u - - - - é vi - - - lai - - - ne, Mar - - got, Je
En re - - - ve - - - nant de Lor - - - rai - - - ne, Mar - - - - - - - got,
Ils m'ont sal - - - u - - - - é vi - - - lai - - - ne, Mar - - - - - - - got,
En re - - - ve - - - nant de Lor - - - rai - - - ne, Mar - - - - - - got,
Ils m'ont sal - - - u - - - - é vi - - - lai - - - ne, Mar - - - - - - got,

14
Ren - con - trai trois ca - - pi - - tai - - nes,
Je suis leur fi - - - è - - vre quar - taine,
vi - - gnes, vi - - gnes, vi - - gno - let,
- con - trai trois ca - - - - - - pi - - tai - - nes,
suis leur fi - - è - - - - - - - vre quar - taine,
vi - gnes, vi - - gnes, vi - - gno - let, Mar -
vi - - gnes, vi - - gnes, vi - - gno - let,

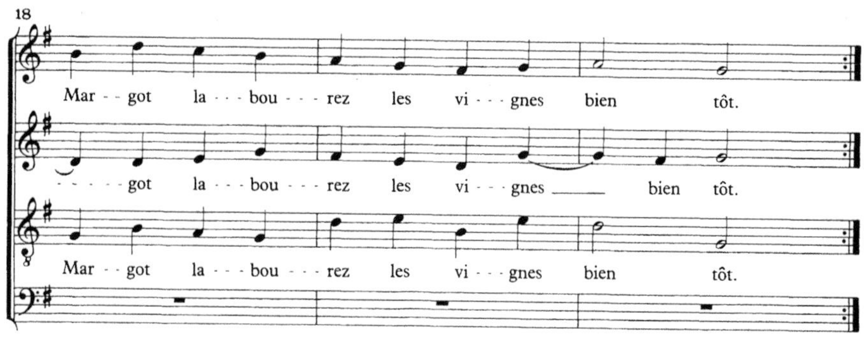
18
Mar - - got la - - - bou - - - rez les vi - - - gnes bien tôt.
- - - - got la - - - bou - - - rez les vi - - gnes bien tôt.
Mar - - got la - - - bou - - - rez les vi - - - gnes bien tôt.

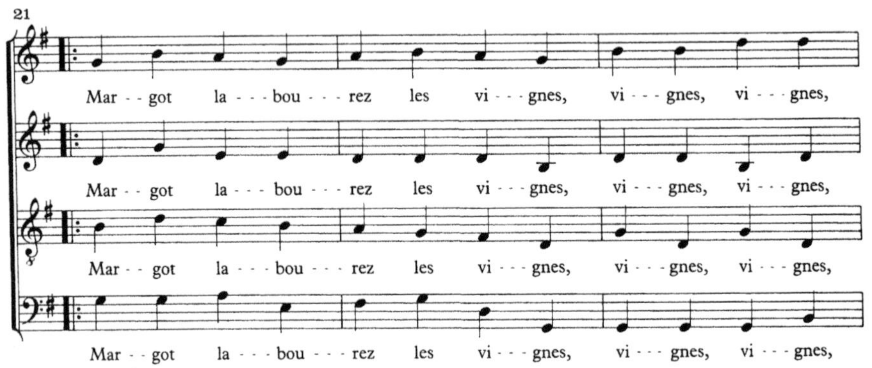
21
Mar - - got la - - - bou - - - rez les vi - - - gnes, vi - - - gnes, vi - - - gnes,
Mar - - got la - - - bou - - - rez les vi - - - gnes, vi - - - gnes, vi - - - gnes,
Mar - - got la - - - bou - - - rez les vi - - - gnes, vi - - - gnes, vi - - - gnes,
Mar - - got la - - - bou - - - rez les vi - - - gnes, vi - - - gnes, vi - - - gnes,

24
Fine
vi - - gno - let, Mar - - - - got la - - bou - - rez les vi - - gnes bien tôt.
vi - - gno - let, Mar - - - - - got la - - bou - - rez les vi - - gnes bien tôt.
vi - - gno - let, Mar - got la - - bou - - - rez les vi - - gnes bien tôt.
vi - - gno - - let, Mar - got la - - bou - - - rez les vi - - gnes bien tôt.

28
3. Ils m'ont don - - né pour é - - - tren - - ne, Mar - - - - - - - - got,
4. S'il fleu - - rit je se - - - rai rei - - - ne, Mar - - - - - - - - got,
3. Ils m'ont don - - né pour é - - - tren - - ne, Mar - - - - - - - - got,
4. S'il fleu - - rit je se - - rai rei - - - ne, Mar - - - - - - - - - got,

31
Ils m'ont don - - - né pour é - - - tren - - - ne, Mar - - - - - - got,
S'il fleu - - rit je se - - - rai rei - - - ne, Mar - - - - - - got,
Ils m'ont don - - né pour é - - - tren - - - ne, Mar - - got, Un
S'il fleu - - - rit je se - - - rai rei - - - ne, Mar - - got, S'il
Ils m'ont don - - - né pour é - - - tren - - - ne, Mar - - - - - - got,
S'il fleu - - rit je se - - - rai rei - - - ne, Mar - - - - - - got,
Ils m'ont don - - né pour é - - - tren - - - ne, Mar - - - - - - got,
S'il fleu - - rit je se - - - rai rei - - - ne, Mar - - - - - - got,

34
Un bou - quet de mar - jo - - lai - - ne,
S'il y meurt je perds ma pei - - ne,
vi - gnes, vi - gnes, vi - gno - let,
bou - quet de mar - - - - - jo - - lai - - ne,
y meurt je perds ma pei - - ne,
vi - gnes, vi - gnes, vi - gno - let, Mar -
vi - gnes, vi - gnes, vi - gno - let,

38
Mar - - got la - - - bou - - - rez les vi - - gnes bien tôt.
- - - - got la - - - bou - - - rez les vi - - gnes bien tôt.
Mar - - got la - - - bou - - - rez les vi - - gnes bien tôt.

15. Un gentil amoureux

CLAUDE LE JEUNE
(c.1530 - 1600)

Chant à 4
1. Tant que loin de ton oeil, sou - - las de mon coeur,
2. Un mo - ment je te - - - - nais pour un très long jour,
1. Tant que loin de ton oeil, sou - - las de mon coeur,
2. Un mo - ment je te - - - - nais pour un très long jour,
1. Tant que loin ___ de ton ___ oeil, sou - - las de mon coeur,
2. Un mo - ment ___ je te - - - - nais pour un très long jour,
1. Tant que loin ___ de ___ ton oeil, sou - - las de mon coeur,
2. Un mo - ment ___ je ___ te - - - - nais pour un très long jour,
Mes beaux ans je cou - - lais, je n'eu que lan - - - gueur,
Au jour seul je trou - - vais du mois le long tour,
Mes beaux ans je cou - - lais, je n'eu que lan - - - gueur,
Au jour seul je trou - - vais du mois le long tour,
Mes ___ beaux ans je cou - - lais, je n'eu que lan - - - gueur,
Au ___ jour seul je trou - - vais du mois le long tour,
Mes beaux ans je cou - - lais, je n'eu que lan - - - gueur,
Au jour seul je trou - - vais du mois le long tour,
Tou - jours maus Et ja - - mais re - - pos.
Et un mois Pour un an j'a - - vais.
Tou - jours maus Et ja - - mais re - - pos.
Et un mois Pour un an j'a - - vais.
Tou - jours maus Et ja - - mais ___ re - - pos.
Et un mois Pour un an ___ j'a - - vais.
Tou - jours maus Et ja - - mais re - - pos.
Et un mois Pour un an j'a - - vais.
A "Rechant à 4" ou "Reprise à 6"

Rechant à 4
Un gen - - - til a - mou - reux sa nim - - - - - - fe é - car - - - - tant De - -
- vient vieil tout à l'in - stant.
Reprise à 6
Un gen - - - - til a - mou-reux sa
nim - - - - fe é - - car - - - - - - tant De - - vient vieil tout à l'in - - stant.

Chant à 4
3. Or de - - puis que mon heur nous a ras - - sem - - - blé,
4. Qu'on ne lais - - - - - - - - se le temps se pas - - - - ser en vain,
3. Or de - - puis que mon heur nous a ras - - sem - - - blé,
4. Qu'on ne lais - - - - - - - - se le temps se pas - - - - ser en vain,
3. Or de - - puis que mon heur nous a ras - - sem - - - blé,
4. Qu'on ne lais - - - - - - - - se le temps se pas - - - - ser en vain,
3. Or de - - puis que mon heur nous a ras - - sem - - - blé,
4. Qu'on ne lais - - - - - - - - se le temps se pas - - - - ser en vain,
D'un grand ai - - - - se je suis tou - - - - jours com - - - - blé;
Gou - - - - - tons l'ai - - - - se pré - - sent et d'un si grand bien
D'un grand ai - - - - se je suis tou - - - - jours com - - - - blé;
Gou - - - - - tons l'ai - - - - se pré - - sent et d'un si grand bien
D'un grand ai - - - - se je suis tou - - - - jours com - - - - blé;
Gou - - - - - tons l'ai - - - - se pré - - sent et d'un si grand bien
D'un grand ai - - - - se je suis tou - - - - jours com - - - - blé;
Gou - - - - - tons l'ai - - - - se pré - - sent et d'un si grand bien
Tout con - - - tent Et ja - - mais do - - lent.
Qui tôt fuit, Pos - - se - - dons le fruit.
A "Rechant à 4"
ou "Reprise à 6"
Tout con - - - tent Et ja - - mais do - - lent.
Qui tôt fuit, Pos - - se - - dons le fruit.
Tout con - - - tent Et ja - - mais do - - lent.
Qui tôt fuit, Pos - - se - - dons le fruit.
Tout con - - - tent Et ja - - mais do - - lent.
Qui tôt fuit, Pos - - se - - dons le fruit.

16. Il est bel et bon

PIERRE PASSEREAU
(fl.1509 - 1547)

11
- ys, Il est bel et bon, bon,
d'un pa - - ys,
Di - - sant l'une à l'au - tre: a - - - vez bon ma - - - - ri? Il est bel et
Di - - - sant l'une à l'au - tre: a - - - - vez bon ma - - - ri?

15
bon, bon, bon, com - - - - mè - - re, il est bel et bon, bon,
Il est bel et bon, bon, bon, bon, bon, com - - mè - - - - - - - - - re,
bon, bon, bon, bon, bon, com - mè - - - - - - - re, il est bel et
Il est bel et bon, bon, bon, com - - mè - - - - - - - - - re,

18
bon, bon, bon, com - - - mè - re, com-mè - re, com - mè - re, mon ma - - ri. Il ne
il est bel et bon, bon, bon, com - mè - re, com - mè - re, mon ma - - ri.
bon, bon, bon, com - - - mè - - - - - re, com - - - mè - - - re, mon ma - - ri.
il est bel et bon, bon, bon, com - - - mè - re, mon ma - - ri.

22
me cour - - rou - ce, ne me bat aus - si.
Il ne me cour - - rou - ce, ne me bat aus - - - - si.
Il ne me cour - - rou - ce,
Il ne me cour -

26
Il fait le mé - - na - ge; Il donne aux pou - -
Il fait le mé - - na - ge;
ne me bat aus - si. Il fait le mé - - - na - ge;
- rou - ce, ne me bat aus - - - - - si. Il fait

30
- lail - les, il donne aux pou - - - lail - les, Et je prends mes
Il donne aux pou - - lail - les, Et je prends mes
Il donne aux pou - - - lail - les, Et je prends mes
le mé - - na - ge; Il donne aux pou - lail - les, Et je prends

34
plai - - - - - - - - sirs. Com - mè - - - - - - - - re, c'est pour ri - - - - - - re,
plai - - - - - - - - - - - - - - sirs. Com - mè - - - - - - - - - - re, c'est pour
plai - - - - sirs. Com - mè - - - - - - - re, c'est pour ri - - - - - -
mes plai - - - - sirs. Com - - - - - mè - - - - - re,

38
Quand les pou - - lail - - - les cri - - - - - - - ent, quand
ri - - - - - re, Quand les pou - - - lail - - - les cri - - - - - -
- re, Quand les pou - - lail - - - - les cri - - - - - - ent,
c'est pour ri - - - - - - - re, Quand les pou - - lail - - - les

42
les pou - lail - - - - - - les cri - ent: Pe - - ti - - te co - quet - - te, pe - ti - - - te co -
- ent: co co co co co co co co co co co dac, co co
quand les pou - - - lail - - - - les cri - - ent: Pe - - - ti - - - te co-quet - - te, pe -
cri - - - - ent: co co co co co dac, co co dac, co co co co co co

46
- quet - - te, pe - ti - - - te co - quet - - te, pe - ti - - te co - quet - - - - - - - - te, qu'est - ce ci ?
co co co co co co dac, co co co co dac, pe - - - - ti - - te co - quet - - te, qu'est- ce ci ?
- ti - - - te co - quet - te, pe - - ti - - - te co-quet - te, pe - ti - - te co - quet - - te, qu'est-ce ci ?
dac, co co co co co co dac, co co dac, pe - - - ti - - te co - quet - - te, qu'est-ce ci ?

50
Il est bel et bon, bon, bon, bon, bon, bon, com - - - mè - re, il est bel et bon, bon,
Il est bel et bon, bon, bon, bon, bon, com - mè - - - - - re,
Il est bel et bon, bon, bon, bon, bon, com - mè - - - - - re, il est bel et
Il est bel et bon, bon, bon, com - mè - - - - - re,

54
bon, bon, bon, com - - - mè - re, com-mè - re, com - mè - - re, mon ma - - - ri.
il est bel et bon, bon, bon, com - - mè - re, com - mè - re, mon ma - - - ri.
bon, bon, bon, com - - - mè - - - - - - re, com - - - mè - - - re, mon ma - - - ri.
il est bel et bon, bon, bon, com - - - mè - re, mon ma - - - ri.

17. Fair Phyllis I saw sitting

JOHN FARMER
(fl.1600)

15
- ver, but af - - ter her lo - ver A - myn - tas hied,
- ver, but af - - ter her lo - ver A - myn - - - tas hied,
- ver, but af - ter her lo-ver A - myn - tas hied, Up and down he
- - - - ver, but af - - ter her lo-ver A - myn - tas hied, Up and

19
Up and down he wandered, up and down he wandered,
Up and down, up and down he wandered, up and down he wan - - - - -
wan - - - - dered, up and down, up and down he wandered, up and down he
down he wan - - - - - - - dered, he wan - - - - - - - - - - - - dered,

23
up and down he wandered, up and down he wandered, up and down
- dered, up ___ and down he wandered, up and down he wan - - - - - - - -
wan - - - dered, up and down he wandered, up and down he wandered,
up and down he

27
he wan - - - - - - dered whilst she was miss - ing; When he found
-dered, he wan - - - dered whilst she was miss-ing; When he found
up and down he wan - - dered whilst she was miss-ing; When he found
wan - - - - - - - - dered whilst she was miss-ing; When he found

32
her, oh then they fell a - - - -
her, oh then they fell a - - - - - kiss - ing, oh then they fell a - - - -
her, oh then they fell a - - - - - kiss - ing, oh then they fell a - - - -
her, oh then they fell a - - - - - kiss - ing, oh then they fell a - - - -

36
1.
2.
- kiss - - ing, a - kiss - - ing, oh then they fell a - - - - - kiss - - ing, - kiss - - ing.
- kiss - - ing, a - kiss - - ing, oh then they fell a - - - - - kiss - - - - ing, - kiss - - ing.
- kiss - - ing, a - kiss - ing, oh then they fell a - - - - kissing. Up and down he - kiss - - ing.
- kiss - ing, a - kiss - ing, oh then they fell a - - - - - kiss - - - - ing. Up and - kiss - - ing.

18. Heigh ho! 'chill go to plough no more

JOHN MUNDY
(c.1555 - 1630)

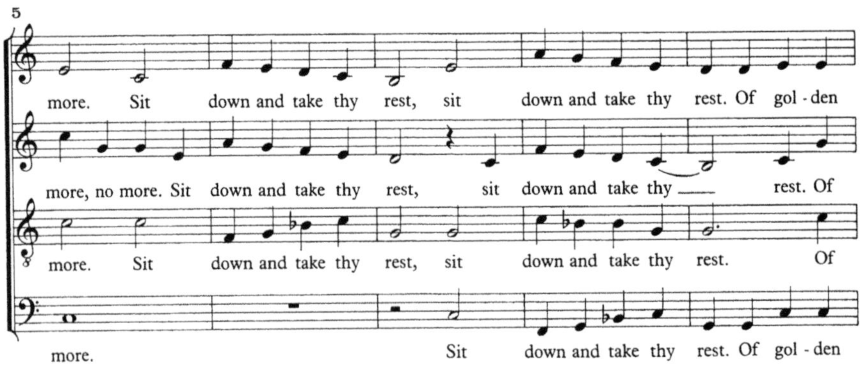

15
flaunt it with the ___ best. But I love, and I love, I ___
it, to flaunt it with the best. But I love, and I
it, to flaunt it with the ___ best. But I love, and I love, and I
to flaunt it with the best. But I love, and I love, I

20
love, and who think you, and who think you?
love, and who think you, and who think you?
love, and who think you, and who think you? The
love, and who think you, and who think you? The

25
The fi - - - - nest lass that e'er you
The fi - - - - nest lass that e'er you knew, the fi - - - - nest lass that e'er you
fi - - -nest lass that e'er you knew, the fi -nest lass that e'er you
fi - - -nest lass that e'er you knew, the fi - -nest lass that e'er you

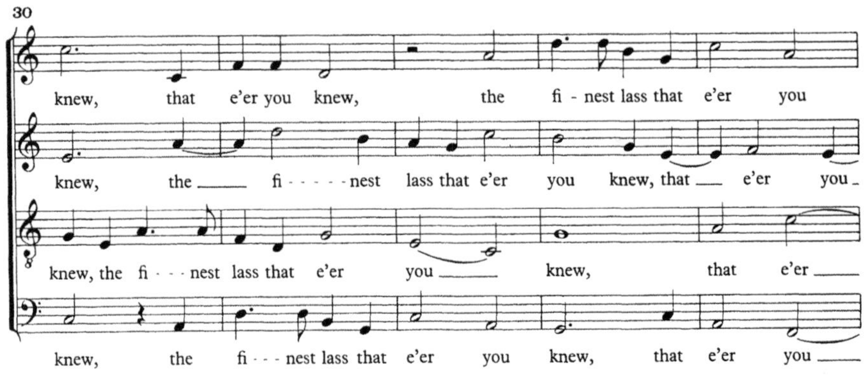
30
knew, that e'er you knew, the fi - nest lass that e'er you
knew, the fi - - - - - nest lass that e'er you knew, that e'er you
knew, the fi - - - nest lass that e'er you knew, that e'er
knew, the fi - - - nest lass that e'er you knew, that e'er you

35
knew; Which makes me sing when I should
knew; Which makes me sing when I should
you knew; Which makes me sing when I should
knew; Which makes me sing when I should

40
cry, Heigh
cry, Heigh ho! for love I die, heigh
cry, Heigh ho! for love I die, heigh
cry, Heigh ho! for love I die,

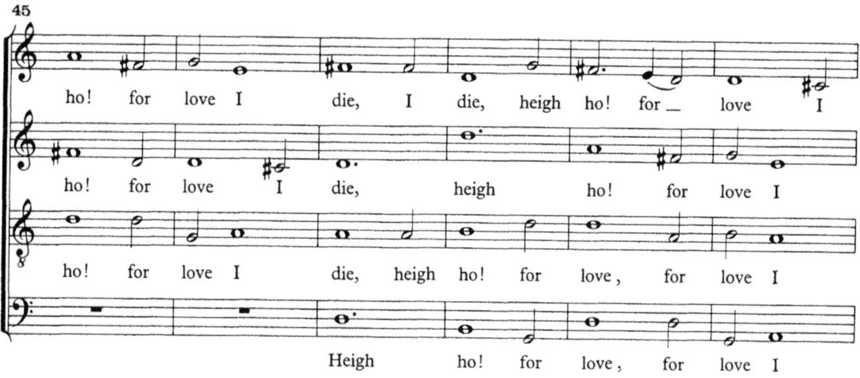
45
ho! for love I die, I die, heigh ho! for _ love I
ho! for love I die, heigh ho! for love I
ho! for love I die, heigh ho! for love, for love I
Heigh ho! for love, for love I

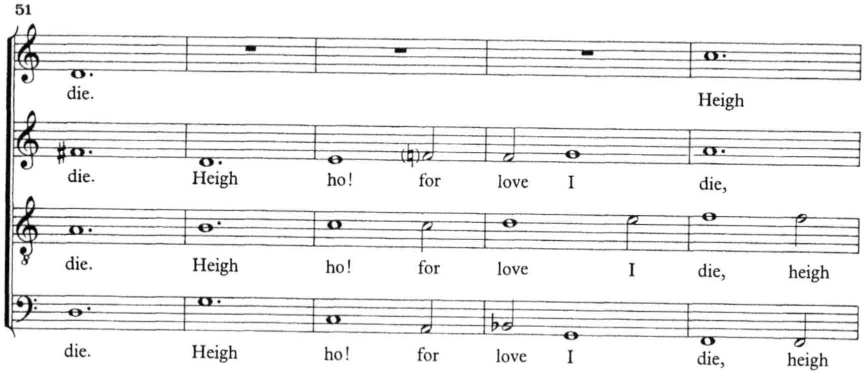
51
die. Heigh
die. Heigh ho! for love I die,
die. Heigh ho! for love I die, heigh
die. Heigh ho! for love I die, heigh

56
ho! for love I die, heigh ho! for _ love I die.
heigh ho! for love I die.
ho! for love I die, heigh ho! for love I die.
ho! for love I die, heigh ho! for love I die.

19. Fine knacks for ladies

JOHN DOWLAND
(1562 - 1626)

9
I keep a fair but for the fair to view:
It is a pre - - - - - - - cious jew - ell to be plain:
But in my heart, where du - - ty serves and loves:
I keep a fair but for the fair to view:
It is a pre - - - - - - - cious jew - ell to be plain:
But in my heart, where du - - ty serves and loves:
I keep a fair but for the fair to view:
It is a pre - - - - - - - cious jew - ell to be plain:
But in my heart, where du - - ty serves and loves:
I keep a fair but for the fair to view:
It is a pre - - - - - - - cious jew - ell to be plain:
But in my heart, where du - - ty serves and loves:

13
A beg - - - - gar may be li - - be - - ral of love.
Some - times in shell th'or - - - - - - i - - enst pearls we find.
Tur - tles and twins, court's brood, a heav'n - ly pair.
A beg - gar may be li - - be - - ral of love.
Some - - - times in shell th'or - - i - - enst pearls we find.
Tur - - - - tles and twins, court's brood, a heav'n - ly pair.
A beg - - - gar may be li - - be - - ral of love.
Some-times in shell th'or - - i - - enst pearls we find.
Tur - tles and twins, court's brood, a heav'n - - - ly pair.
A beg - gar may be li - - be - - ral of love.
Some - - - times in shell th'or - - i - - enst pearls we find.
Tur - - - - tles and twins, court's brood, a heav'n - - - ly pair.

17
Though all my wares be trash, the heart is true,
Of o - - thers take a sheaf, of me a grain,
Hap - - - py the heart that thinks of no re - moves,
Though all my wares be trash, the heart is true, the
Of o - - thers take a sheaf, of me a grain, of
Hap - - - - - py the heart that thinks of no re - moves, of
Though all my wares be trash, the heart, the heart is true, the
Of o - - thers take a sheaf, of me, of me a grain, of
Hap - - - - - py the heart that thinks, that thinks of no re - moves, that
Though all my wares be trash, the heart is true, is true, the
Of o - - thers take a sheaf, of me a grain, of me, of
Hap - - - - - py the heart that thinks of no re - moves, that thinks of

23
the heart is true, the heart is true.
of me a grain, of me a grain!
of no re - moves, of no re - - - - moves.
heart is true, the heart is true, is true.
me a grain, of me a grain, a grain!
no re - - - moves, of no re - - moves, re - - - - - - moves.
heart, the heart is true, is true, the heart is true, the heart is true.
me, of me a grain, of me, of me a grain, of me a grain!
thinks of no re - - moves, that thinks of no re - - moves, of no re - moves.
heart is true, the heart is true, the heart is true.
me a grain, of me a grain, of me a grain!
no re - - - moves, of no re - moves, of no re - - moves.

20. Of all the birds that I do know

GEORGE GASCOIGNE
(1539 - 1577)

JOHN BARTLET
(fl.1610)

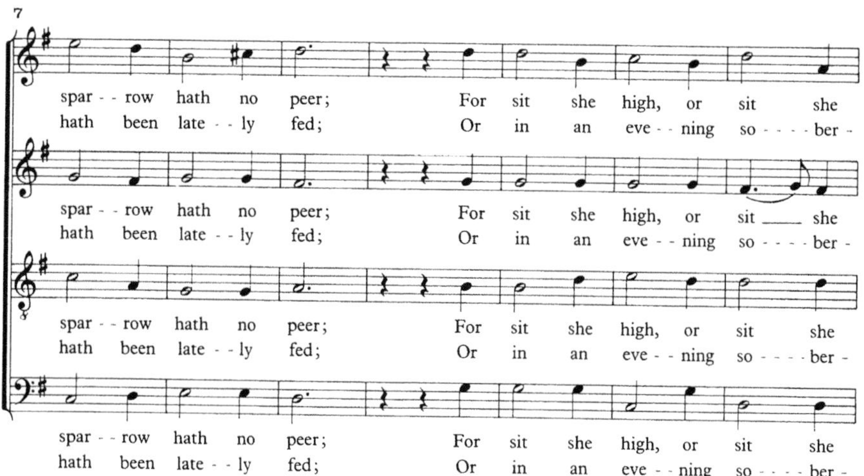

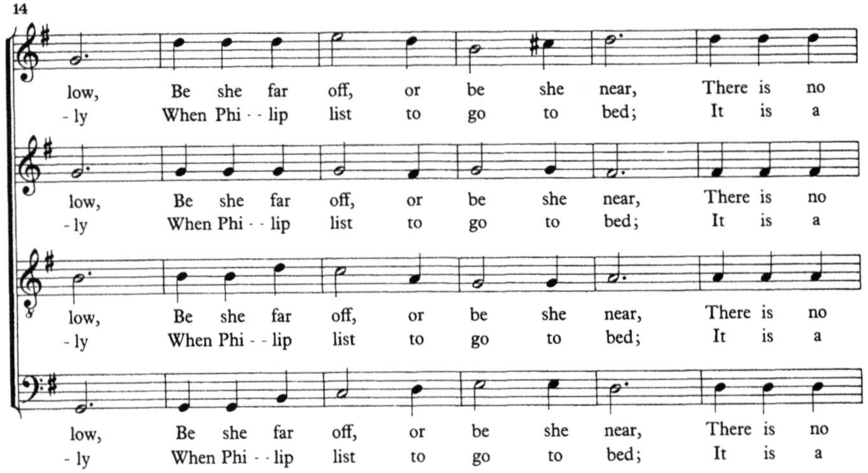
14
low, Be she far off, or be she near, There is no
-ly When Phi - - lip list to go to bed; It is a
low, Be she far off, or be she near, There is no
-ly When Phi - - lip list to go to bed; It is a
low, Be she far off, or be she near, There is no
-ly When Phi - - lip list to go to bed; It is a
low, Be she far off, or be she near, There is no
-ly When Phi - - lip list to go to bed; It is a

20
bird so fair, so fine, Nor yet so fresh as this of mine;
heaven to hear my Phipp, How she can chirp with mer - - ry lip,
bird so fair, so fine, Nor yet so fresh as this of mine;
heaven to hear my Phipp, How she can chirp with mer - - ry lip,
bird so fair, so fine, Nor yet so fresh as this of mine;
heaven to hear my Phipp, How she can chirp with mer - - ry lip,
bird so fair, so fine, Nor yet so fresh as this of mine;
heaven to hear my Phipp, How she can chirp with mer - - ry lip,

27
For when she once hath felt the fit, Phi - lip will cry still:
For when she once hath felt the fit, Phi - lip will cry still:
For when she once hath felt the fit, Phi - lip will cry still:
For when she once hath felt the fit, Phi - lip will cry still:

34
yet, yet, yet, yet, yet, yet, yet, yet, yet, yet, yet, yet, yet, yet.
yet, yet, yet, yet, yet, yet, yet, yet, yet, yet, yet, yet, yet, yet, yet, yet.
yet, yet, yet, yet, yet, yet, yet, yet, yet, yet, yet, yet, yet, yet, yet.
yet, yet, yet, yet, yet, yet, yet, yet, yet, yet, yet, yet, yet, yet, yet.

40
3. She ne - - - ver wan - - ders far a - - broad, But is at
4. And yet be - - sides all this good sport My Phi - lip
5. And to tell truth he were to blame, Hav - ing so

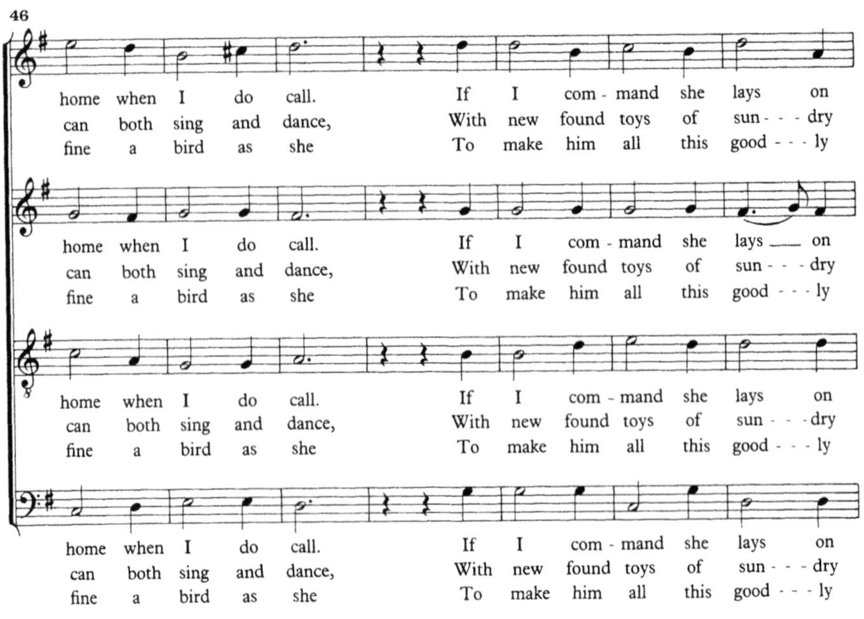
46
home when I do call. If I com - mand she lays on
can both sing and dance, With new found toys of sun - - - dry
fine a bird as she To make him all this good - - - ly

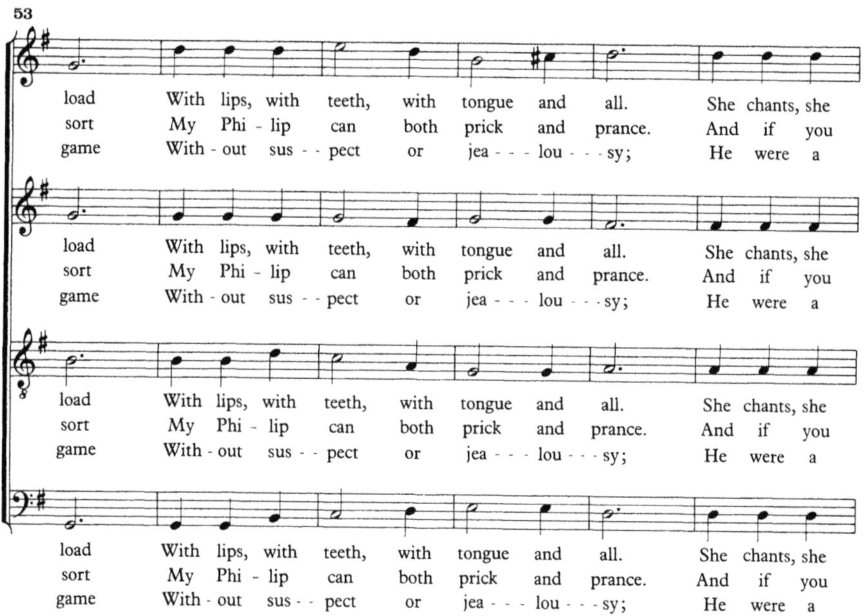
53
load With lips, with teeth, with tongue and all. She chants, she
sort My Phi - lip can both prick and prance. And if you
game With - out sus - - pect or jea - - - lou - - - sy; He were a
load With lips, with teeth, with tongue and all. She chants, she
sort My Phi - lip can both prick and prance. And if you
game With - out sus - - pect or jea - - - lou - - - sy; He were a
load With lips, with teeth, with tongue and all. She chants, she
sort My Phi - lip can both prick and prance. And if you
game With - out sus - - pect or jea - - - lou - - - sy; He were a
load With lips, with teeth, with tongue and all. She chants, she
sort My Phi - lip can both prick and prance. And if you
game With - out sus - - pect or jea - - - lou - - - sy; He were a

59
D.𝄋
chirps, she makes such cheer, That I be - - lieve she hath no peer.
say but: fend cut, Phipp! Lord, how the peat will turn and skip!
churl and knew no good, Would see her faint for lack of food,
chirps, she makes such cheer, That I be - - lieve she hath no peer.
say but: fend cut, Phipp! Lord, how the peat will turn and skip!
churl and knew no good, Would see her faint for lack of food,
chirps, she makes such cheer, That I be - - lieve she hath no peer.
say but: fend cut, Phipp! Lord, how the peat will turn and skip!
churl and knew no good, Would see her faint for lack of food,
chirps, she makes such cheer, That I be - - lieve she hath no peer.
say but: fend cut, Phipp! Lord, how the peat will turn and skip!
churl and knew no good, Would see her faint for lack of food,

21. Adieu, sweet Amaryllis

JOHN WILBYE
(1574 - 1638)

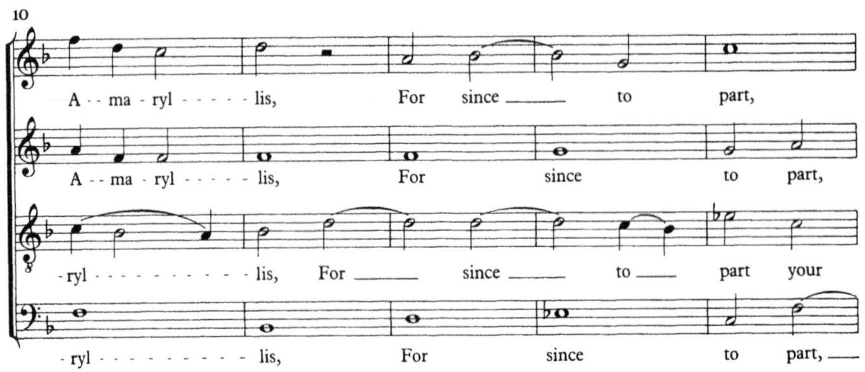

15
to part your will is, O heavy tid-
to part your will is, O hea-vy tid-
will is, O hea-vy
your will is, O hea-vy tid-

21
-ing, Here is for me no bid-ing. Yet
-ing, Here is for me, here is for me no bid-ing. Yet
tid-ing, Here is for me no bid-ing. Yet once a-
-ing, Here is for me no bid-ing. Yet

26
once a-gain, yet once a-gain, a-gain, ere that I part with you, yet
once a-gain, a-gain, ere that I part with you,
-gain, yet once a-gain, a-gain, ere that I part with you, yet once a
once a-gain, a-gain, ere that I part with you, yet

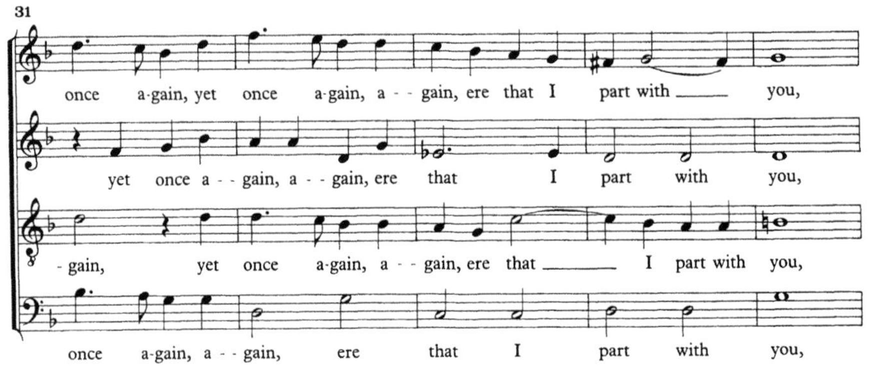
31
once a-gain, yet once a-gain, a - - gain, ere that I part with ___ you,
yet once a - - gain, a - - gain, ere that I part with you,
- gain, yet once a-gain, a - - gain, ere that ___ I part with you,
once a-gain, a - - gain, ere that I part with you,

36
A - ma - ryl - lis, A - ma-ryl - lis sweet, a - - - - dieu, a - dieu, a - dieu,
A - ma - ryl - lis, A - ma-ryl - lis sweet, a - - - - dieu, a - - dieu, a - -
A - ma - ryl - lis, A - ma-ryl - lis sweet, a - - dieu, a - - dieu, a - - dieu, a - -
A - ma - ryl - lis, A - ma-ryl - lis sweet, a-dieu, a - - dieu, a - - dieu, a - -

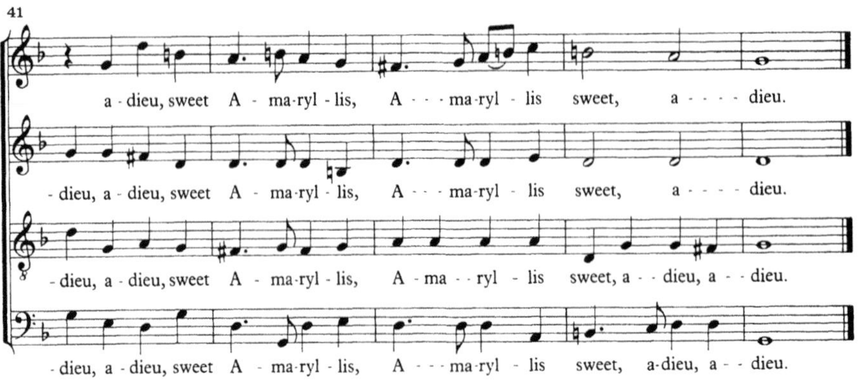
41
a - dieu, sweet A - ma-ryl - lis, A - - - ma-ryl - lis sweet, a - - - - dieu.
- dieu, a - dieu, sweet A - ma-ryl - lis, A - - - ma-ryl - lis sweet, a - - - - dieu.
- dieu, a - dieu, sweet A - ma-ryl - lis, A - ma - - ryl - lis sweet, a - - dieu, a - - dieu.
- dieu, a - dieu, sweet A - ma-ryl - lis, A - - - ma-ryl - lis sweet, a-dieu, a - - dieu.

EDITORIAL NOTES

This performing edition aims to present the music in notation that will be readily understood by singers today. Word texts have been carefully edited and presented in modern orthography. Since all pieces except no. 9 are available in standard musicological editions, it has not been thought necessary to print a detailed critical commentary. Editorial accidentals are printed in small type, and all accidentals apply throughout the bar. For each piece, the following information is set out below: source|original clefs|original key signature|original time signature|the note reduction adopted in this edition (if applicable)|the degree of transposition (if applicable)|principal variants. Minor adjustments — such as correcting obvious errors and adjusting note lengths of final chords — have been made tacitly.

Clefs are abbreviated as follows:

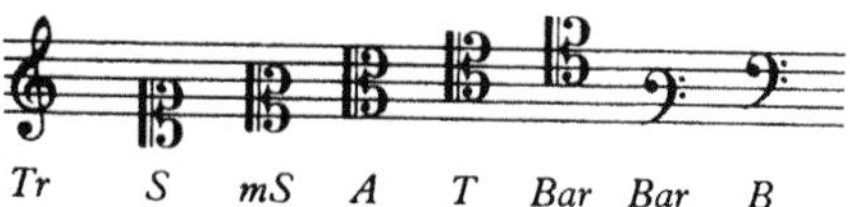

1–3. Cancionero Musical de Palacio (Madrid, Palacio Real, 2–I–5)
1. *S mS T B*|none|¢3 ¢|¼
2. *S mS A Bar*|*S* B♭; *mS* bar 1 E♭, bar 11 B♭; *A* B♭; *Bar* B♭ E♭|none|¼|Black notation. *Bar* bar 13 (&17) ♪♩ ♩ ♪
3. *S A T B*|♭|¢3|½
4. Vásquez: Villancicos y Canciones, 1551. *Tr S mS T*|none|C|½|down tone
5. 121 newe Lieder, 1534. *Tr A A Bar*|♭|¢3|¼

6–7. Teutscher Liedlein II, 1540
6. *S A T B*|♭|¢|½|up tone|bar 2 original text 'eo' (= to him). 'Deo' is more effective: the letter 'D' could well have been a hand-decorated initial, omitted at some stage in the transmission of the piece.
7. *S A A Bar*|♭|¢|½|up tone
8. Frotole libro secondo, 1505. *mS A A B*|none|C|½|up tone|*A1* & *A2* exchanged except for bars 11–12, 20–36, 40–41
9. Seville, Bibl. Columbina 5–I–43. *Tr A A T*|none|bar 1 C; bar 10 (moved to bar 11) ¢; bar 27 ¢3; bar 56 ¢|½ (bar 1–10); ¼ (bar 11–59)|down tone|*A1* & *A2* exchanged except for bars 12–5, 19–26, 43–5, 46–7, 51–2. While the Seville MS is the prime source, features are taken from Paris, Bibl. Nat. Res. Vm^7 676 f36v (also consulted were I Fn Panc. 27 f43v, D-ddr LEu Ms 1494 f247v)
10. Arcadelt: Il primo libro, 1539. *mS A T B*|♭|¢|up tone
11. Lassus: Libro de villanelle, 1581. *S A T B*|♭|C
12. 31 Chansons, 1529. *Tr mS A Bar*|♭|¢|½|down tone|*mS* & *A* exchanged bars 19–21
13. Tiers livre contenant 29 chansons, 1540. *S A A Bar*|*S* & *A2* B♭; *A1* & *Bar* B♭ E♭|¢|½
14. Tiers livre de chansons, 1554. *S A T B*|♭|¢|½|up tone
15. Le Jeune: Airs, 1608. *S S A T T B*|♭|C|up tone
16. 28 chansons musicales, 1534. *S A T B*|none|¢|½|up tone|*A* bars 47 (last note) — 48 'co co dac, mon ami'
17. Farmer: Madrigals, 1599. *S mS T B*| |C C
18. Mundy: Songs and psalms, 1594. *Tr Tr mS Bar*|♭|¢|down fourth
19. Dowland: The second booke of songs or ayres, 1600. *Tr mS A B*|♭|C
20. Bartlet: A Book of ayres, 1604. *S mS A B*|none|3|*A* bar 5 first two notes changed from D to B (to provide a third in the chord, which is in the omitted lute part)
21. Wilbye: The first set of English madrigals, 1598. *S mS A B* |♭|C

Clifford Bartlett

PRONUNCIATION GUIDE

	FRENCH	GERMAN
a	**up**; before final s = father; à = **up**; â = father; ai = **let** except at end of word = late; au = **rope**. See also note 3 below.	father; before 2 consonants = **up**; ä = late; au = **owl**
e	before consonant in same syllable or 2 consonants = **let**; at end of syllable = **garden**; final unstressed e, es, ent = garden; è, ê = **let**; é = late; eau = **rope**; ei = **let**; eu, eû = mouthshape for 'oh' but say 'ee'. See also note 3 below	late; before 2 consonants or at end of word = **let**; ei = **height**; eu = **oil**
i	**feet**; before vowel = **year**. See also note 3 below.	**feet**; before 2 consonants = wind; ie = **feet**
o	**cause**; before s and at end of word = **rope**; ô = **rope**; oeu = mouthshape for 'oh' but say 'ee'; oi = **wah**; ou = **soon** except before vowel = **w**. See also note 3 below	**rope**; before 2 consonants = **pause**
u	u, û = mouthshape for 'oo' but say 'ee'; before vowel = **year**. See also note 3 below	**soon**; before 2 consonants = **put**; ü = French **u**
b	before c, s, t = **p**	at end of word = **p**
c	**k** except before e, i, y = **ss**; ç = **ss**; ch = **shame**	**k**; ch = lo**ch** (Scottish)
d		at end of word = **t**
g	**go** except before e, i, y = **vision**; gn = **onion**	**go** except at end of word = **k**
h	usually silent	silent after vowel
j	**vision**	**year**
l	after i and at end of word = **year**	
nt	usually silent at end of word	
qu	**k**	**kv**
s	**ss** except between vowels or when elided = **z**; silent at end of word; est = **eh** (silent 'st')	**ss** except before vowel = **z**; sch = **shame**; at start of syllable sp = **shp**, st = **sht**
th	**t**	**t**
v		**f**
w		**v**
x	silent at end of word	
y	**feet** except before vowel = **year**	
z		**its**

NOTES

1. Consonants sound as in English unless indicated otherwise. Double consonants in Italian are given extra stress.
2. Vowels in English are often sounded as diphthongs, e.g. *I may go* = *ai mei gou*. In other languages vowels sounds must be kept constant for their full duration.
3. In French the letter *m* or *n* after a vowel or diphthong is not sounded but makes the vowel nasal, i.e. adds a touch of *ng*. (The same applies sometimes to *nt* at the end of a word.) The following are all nasalized: *am, an, ean, em, en* = **ah**; *aim, ain, eim, ein, im, in* = **eh**; *ien, yen* = **ee-eh**; *om, on* = **oh**; *oin* = **weh**; *um, un* = mouthshape for 'aw' but say 'eh'.
4. French is often liased. When the ensuing word begins with a vowel, sound the final consonant of the previous word even if it is usually silent: *Elle est ici avec un homme* would sound *elleteesseeavecunom*.
5. In Italian and Spanish, all vowels must be pronounced, even when two are written to be sung on one note.
6. Accents on vowels in Italian and Spanish indicate stress and do not change the sound.